Making partnerships work

A practical guide for the public, private, voluntary and community sectors

Andrew Wilson and Kate Charlton

The **Joseph Rowntree Foundation** has supported this project as part of its programme of research and innovative development projects, which it hopes will be of value to policy makers and practitioners. The facts presented and views expressed in this report are, however, those of the authors and not necessarily those of the Foundation.

This report has been produced by the Ashridge Research Centre for Business and Society. The focus of the Centre is an investigation into the rapidly changing relationship between public, private and voluntary sector organisations. Within this theme, the Centre conducts research into two interrelated issues: the relationship between corporate competitiveness and accountability to stakeholders; the role of business as stakeholder in society. Current and recent studies include investigations into issues of business ethics, corporate reputation, and the changing nature of corporate community involvement and investment.

© Joseph Rowntree Foundation 1997

All rights reserved.

Published by YPS for the Joseph Rowntree Foundation

ISBN 1 899987 39 8

Prepared and printed by:
York Publishing Services Ltd
64 Hallfield Road
Layerthorpe
York YO3 7XQ

Contents

Acknowledgements

We would like to thank the members of the Advisory Group (listed below) for the advice and support they have given during the study. We are also extremely grateful to all the interviewees who took part in this research – they have provided a fascinating insight into the process of partnership management. Without their help and co-operation, this report would not have been possible.

Anna Abel-Smith, Independent Research Consultant

Virginia Burton, the Voluntary and Community Division of the Department for National Heritage

Ian Christie, Henley Centre for Forecasting

Alan Curless, Hereford and Worcester Training and Enterprise Council

Laurence Handy, Ashridge Research

Amanda Jordan, NatWest Group

John Kaye, Voluntary Action Leeds

Pat Kneen, Joseph Rowntree Foundation

Tony Marshall, the Voluntary and Community Division of the Department for National Heritage

Chris Skelcher, Department of Local Government Studies, the University of Birmingham

Cay Stratton, Business in the Community

Julia Sudbury, Sia

Summary

An overview

The central aim of this report is to illustrate, through practical advice and example, how managers in the public, private and voluntary sectors can work together to develop and maintain cross-sectoral partnerships.

We present a pragmatic appraisal of the barriers that can prevent the partnership process from operating smoothly; and put forward strategies for overcoming these hurdles. These strategies are drawn from the experiences of the 12 partnerships we studied, in total some 60 individuals who have walked down this rocky path. We highlight those issues that need to be taken into consideration by individuals or organisations that are already operating in, or might be considering entering into, a partnership initiative.

One of the key lessons of this report is that partnerships will exist for different reasons, create different structures, involve different partners and set themselves different goals. Successful partnerships are aware of their context and the impact this has on the way they must operate in order to develop successful approaches to partnership management. Perhaps the most important variable in this respect is the stage the partnership has reached in its development process. An illustrative model of partnership development is outlined in Chapter 1 (page 16). It is used in this summary to highlight the key issues that need to be considered in a successful partnership management process.

Stage one

The partners come together through the mutual recognition of a common need, or in a joint effort to obtain public funds.

The term partnership can be used to describe a range of initiatives. To be effective, partners must work together to achieve a commonly agreed set of goals and objectives and in so doing deliver more than the sum of its individual components.

One message was repeated by the vast majority of interviewees – there needs to be an acceptance that a partnership approach will add value to the initiative. This point was reinforced by one who suggested that, 'you don't start off with the notion of a partnership for its own sake. You start with a number of interrelated issues and realise that interagency working is the only way to address them.'

If they have not worked together before, the partners begin the process of overcoming differences in backgrounds and approach, building trust and respect.

The objective must be to allow people from very different backgrounds the opportunity to learn about:

- each other

- their organisations

- the pressures and constraints under which they operate

- what each can bring to the partnership

- what each hopes to get out of the partnership.

Partners must make every effort possible to understand the perspective of others involved in the initiative. Be open and honest with others so they can understand what it is you are able to bring to the partnership and, equally important, what you are unable to deliver. Try to achieve this exchange at the outset, in order to build the foundation for equal treatment, equal respect and equal commitment.

The important point for those embarking on this journey is that the partnership development process is not inevitable – it requires time, energy and effort to maintain momentum and drive forward the initiative.

There may be a need for training, building each partner's capacity to operate effectively in this new organisation.

In order to ensure that individuals are able to fulfil their roles, there may be a need for training and development of the partners in some or all of the following areas:

- 'process skills' and 'task skills' to enable the partnership to run efficiently

- knowledge about a wide range of issues from the legal duties of partnerships to information about grant regimes

- confidence and ability to communicate on equal terms with other members of the partnership.

Stage two

Through a process of dialogue and discussion, the partners establish the common ground and work towards agreeing a vision and mission statement for the initiative.

There was almost unanimous agreement amongst interviewees that a shared vision is vital for a partnership to succeed. The acid test for a vision seems to be whether or not it provides an enduring reference point for the partnership – is it something on which the members can reflect when difficult issues have to be resolved, and does it inform decision-making or simply lead to more debate?

A mission statement should:

- bring together all the partners around an agreed set of aspirations

- provide a framework which describes the activities the partnership seeks to undertake (and by implication indicates which activities are excluded)

- outline the specific targets and goals of the partnership

- specify the processes and procedures by which these targets and goals will be achieved

- describe what resources the partnership will utilise.

The original core group of partners might agree on the need to involve more individuals and organisations in the initiative.

A partnership can impact upon a wide range of people and will need to involve different stakeholders at a number of different levels. Such stakeholders are able to influence the success of the partnership – both positively and negatively – either by supporting it or being hostile to its activities.

Initiatives that do not engage and involve members of the community in which they operate run the risk of failure – it is natural for people to feel suspicious of an initiative that is trying to change things in a particular area without any reference to the people living and working in that area.

However, there is a need for balance. Partnerships which spend all their time talking without taking action are also doomed to failure. Several interviewees expressed the fear that, in seeking to be representative, a partnership runs the risk of degenerating into a talking shop.

Where there is choice about who joins the partnership, look for individuals who have the skills and a willingness to contribute, but see them as a gateway into their organisation. Be prepared to include people whose potential contribution is less obvious in order to keep the peace or access vital resources.

The partners develop mechanisms for assessing needs and quantifying the size of the task they propose to undertake.

It is necessary to have an understanding of the area in which the partnership intends to operate. As one interviewee put it, 'you need a fundamental study of the physical, the economic, the environmental and the other problems of a particular area. If you like, what its pathology is, what its opportunities are, what its difficulties are, and what its relationship is with other areas.'

For this process of needs analysis to be meaningful, all partners must have a say in:

- how issues are identified

- how these issues are prioritised

- how actions and objectives are decided upon.

Typically, this process will involve three elements:

- an analysis of published data on relevant social and economic indices

- an analysis of existing provision in terms of what other organisations might be doing to address similar or related issues to those identified by the partnership

- an analysis of the 'target audience' by seeking advice and information directly from those individuals with whom the partnership seeks to work.

The initiative combines the information generated by the needs assessment exercise together with the vision and mission statement to produce an agenda for action.

In developing its agenda, a partnership will need to balance process and outputs. For some, the sole criterion of a successful partnership is one that meets its stated objectives. For others, however, this measure must be tempered by a consideration of the processes by which the aims of the partnership are met.

It is important to balance these two perspectives. At one level, it is quite clear that a partnership that does not deliver a significant proportion of what it set out to achieve cannot be said to be successful. At the other extreme, an initiative that produces real change but does so without the support and involvement of all three sectors cannot be truly described as a partnership – it is simply an entrepreneurial operation.

Stage three

The formal framework and organisational structure of the partnership is designed and put in place.

Most of the partnerships included in this report had, at an early point in their development process, established a formal constitution or legal structure. Generally, this structure provides the framework for decision-making processes and defines the roles and responsibilities of those involved in the governance and management of the partnership.

Whilst partnership structures can vary considerably, the most common organisational structure is one that comprises three discrete elements:

- a governance function – the executive body of the partnership

- a management function – those who are charged with implementing the partnership's activities

- a consultative function – the various committees, subcommittees and steering groups that report to the executive body.

The partners set specific goals, targets and objectives linked into the agenda for action.

The advice of interviewees was that a partnership should aim to develop a 'balanced portfolio' of goals and objectives. At one level, it is important that the initiative is seen to be doing something concrete in the short-term. For this reason, it should seek to establish a number of clearly defined, easily delivered outcomes.

However, whilst a sense of urgency can be a very positive thing, it is important to avoid 'a poverty of aspiration'. Hence, the initiative must also seek to create the bigger vision, pulling together the partnership to produce a major impact on a much wider area.

Where appropriate, the executive arm of the partnership selects or appoints a management team (even if this is one person) to oversee the work of the initiative.

The role of the management team was variously described by interviewees as that of facilitator, co-ordinator, initiator and implementor. In broad terms, its purpose is to implement the agenda that is set by the partnership board by translating the policies of the partnership into specific actions. This is likely to involve functions such as planning, contracting and resource management.

In deciding upon the constitution, framework and organisational structure of the initiative, all partners must be aware of the potential implications of such decisions as where is the management team located, who funds it, and to whom does it report?

The relationship between the board and the management team is the key to ensuring that intentions with regard to representation and accountability are turned into reality. Clarity about the extent to which powers are delegated to the management team is vital. Attention to job titles within management teams can be useful in managing external perceptions as to who leads the partnership.

Stage four

The partnership delivers to its action plan, whether this be service provision or some other function.

There are likely to be two strands to the work of the initiative: the day-to-day functioning of the partnership and the realisation of a 'bigger vision' – producing a major impact by increasing the capacity of those the partnership is working with to 'help themselves'.

In many respects, carrying out the day-to-day operations of the partnership is usually relatively straightforward. What is more difficult is maintaining and developing what has been achieved – ensuring that new assets or resources are not simply 'bolted on' to the communities in which the partnership is working, but take root in a way that enables initial investments to be leveraged and multiply to achieve much wider benefits.

All interviewees agreed that the aim of a partnership initiative should be to move beyond fire-fighting and temporary solutions. A cross-sectoral initiative should have the power and energy to bring about permanent change in the area in which it operates.

Positive publicity can make life much easier for partnerships, facilitating access to funds, other resources and wider involvement. It does not come automatically and needs to be planned for, as with any other aspect of the partnership's activities. But actions speak louder than words, and a record of achievement is, in any case, the key to good PR.

The executive arm seeks to maintain the involvement of all partners, formulates policy decisions and ensures the continuing accountability of the partnership.

Attention needs to be paid to the composition of the board and the means by which all members are enabled to feel equal partners. Decision-making by consensus tends to be favoured in partnerships and helps to increase perceptions of equality of status internally and fair representation externally.

A pragmatic, action-oriented approach to the work of the partnership will bring benefits. Several interviewees stressed that people generally want to be involved in 'making and doing things', as well as planning and designing. One strategy to help overcome apathy and disinterest is to get as many people as possible physically involved in delivering the work of the partnership.

Partners must be aware that any formal organisational structure will inevitably have an informal shadow. A partnership is no different. The skill is to use informal networks, links and alliances to build positive relations between all the different partners. If these informal relations are open and accessible to all, then the process will reinforce the values and ethos of the partnership.

There is an ongoing process of assessing, evaluating and refining the operations of the partnership.

A partnership must develop transparent measures of success (both quantitative and qualitative) that judge the activities of the initiative against its stated aims and objectives. Externally verifiable performance indicators will improve both internal management processes (assuming the information is used as part of a wider process of performance review) and external credibility and accountability.

This process of performance measurement should look outwards as well as inwards. It is vitally important that a partnership should benchmark its activities against other similar initiatives. Partners should be active 'networkers' and build links across and between other initiatives in order to learn from others' experience and improve the general understanding of the issues each seeks to address.

Stage five

Where appropriate, the partners plan their exit strategy. This involves developing a new set of goals for the survival and continuation of the work of the initiative in some form.

It is very important to recognise that part of the successful partnership management process must be a readiness to question the continuing viability of the initiative. Partners must be prepared to ask 'has the partnership, in this particular form, done what it set out to do?' Inevitably, there will come a time when the answer to this question is 'yes' and all partners must have prepared for this eventuality in advance.

Partners seek to create 'life after death' by transferring the assets of the partnership back into the community with which they work.

An essential requirement of any partnership initiative is to develop the knowledge, experience and abilities of the communities in which they operate so that they become self-managing.

The partnership should avoid constructing barriers to community participation and enable community representatives to experience at first hand the various aspects of partnership management. Hence, all partners need to be given the opportunity to develop and acquire the skills to:

- analyse and define the areas and issues to be addressed by the initiative

- prioritise needs

- develop a vision and mission statement

- select partners, advisors and collaborators

- understand the system – know where grants come from and how to access funding and support

- design programmes of action and the appropriate management structures to support them

- implement, monitor and assess programmes

- review and recreate the long-term strategic direction of the initiative.

The 'golden thread' of involvement, consultation and participation remains central if ambitions to create change that outlives the partnership are to be realised. The lessons learned by the partnership on its journey through the development cycle seem likely to be equally applicable to those in community and other groups who seek to build on the partnership's work.

The aims, structures and working methods of the 12 case study partnerships are all quite different, and arguably there is a spectrum of success represented amongst the group. Nonetheless, we have been able to identify enough common ground across the experiences of each initiative to draw some clear conclusions about the processes and approaches that lead to more successful outcomes. We hope that the lessons spelled out in this report will prove valuable to those who are already on, or are seeking to embark upon, the partnership route.

1 Introduction

Aims and objectives

The central aim of this report is to illustrate, through practical advice and example, how managers in the public, private and voluntary sectors can work together to develop and maintain cross-sectoral partnerships. The objective is to examine the process of partnership development by investigating both the factors that contribute to the successful management of cross-sectoral partnerships and those that hinder such initiatives.

The report highlights how differences in the purpose, structure and evolution of a partnership impact upon successful management practices. The findings of the report draw on a series of almost 60 in-depth interviews with senior personnel currently involved in 12 different cross-sectoral partnerships.[1] A brief description of each of these initiatives is contained in Box 1.

Box 1 The partnerships studied

For a more detailed description, see Appendix 2.

Broxtowe Small Area Regeneration Partnership, Nottingham

The Broxtowe estate is a 1930s housing development of some 2,000 homes (6,000 people) on the north-eastern edge of Nottingham city centre. This partnership came out of a general recognition of the need to adopt a multiagency approach to some of the problems of crime, poor housing and lack of employment opportunities on the estate.

The Daycare Trust, London

The Daycare Trust was formed as a charitable organisation in 1989 by the National Childcare Campaign which lobbied for extended provision of public sector nursery care. Through its Childcare Link programme, it provides information and advice, helps to develop childcare facilities, and promotes quality standards in childcare provision in specific local areas.

Ebor Gardens Partnership, Leeds

This partnership was established in 1994 as a business-led initiative that aims to work with the residents of the Ebor Gardens estate on a range of social, economic and environmental projects.

Groundwork, Dearne Valley

Groundwork Dearne Valley is working to improve the environmental, social and economic environment in an area of South Yorkshire that has suffered greatly from the decline of traditional coal and steel industries.

Manchester University Settlement

In 1995, the Manchester University Settlement celebrated its centenary year. Its agenda currently covers a range of issues centred around the themes of community development, young people and housing.

Mansfield Diamond Partnership

This partnership developed in response to the pit closure programme. The concept of the

---

'diamond' comes from the different facets of the initiative which include work in business development, education and training; environmental issues; crime and safety; infrastructure; and a package of measures aimed at Mansfield Woodhouse, a disadvantaged community in the area.

Moss Side and Hulme Community Development Trust, Manchester

The Moss Side and Hulme area of Manchester is home to nearly 40,000 people from a broad range of racial, ethnic and social backgrounds. Set up in the late 1980s it is an independent, non-profit-making, cross-sectoral partnership that has three strategic aims: local wealth creation; community empowerment; and financial independence and self-sufficiency.

The Netherton Partnership, Liverpool

This partnership was established in 1994 and has successfully bid for Single Regeneration Budget (SRB) funds. Its activities comprise education, training and employment; housing; community safety, crime prevention and youth provision; the environment, recreation and leisure; and care, health and community support.

The Sheffield City Liaison Group, Sheffield

This partnership is an enabling and facilitating group; it does not carry out tasks but sets the strategic agenda for the economic and social regeneration of the city. The group comprises senior representatives of Chambers of Commerce and Industry, the City Council, Sheffield Development Corporation, Sheffield Hallam University, Sheffield Health Authority, Sheffield Training and Enterprise Council (TEC), the University of Sheffield and the Company of Cutlers.

Shirebrook District Development Trust, Derbyshire

This partnership was set up in 1994 in response to colliery closures in order to give advice to local people and support for local businesses. The trust is a non-profit-making company, limited by guarantee. Self-sufficiency is an important goal – the trust owns a number of properties throughout the town which generate a significant income stream albeit from low or subsidised rents.

The TRAX Motor Project, Oxford

TRAX grew out of a probationary service initiative that was set up in the summer of 1991 in response to the rise in car crime in the Oxford area. TRAX is a registered charity and a limited company. Its mission is 'to channel the natural enthusiasm of young people for vehicles into a positive and challenging direction, to aid their development towards further achievement'.

Wester Hailes Partnership, Edinburgh

This partnership is one of four area-based initiatives established following the publication in 1988 of the Scottish Office document *New Life for Urban Scotland*. It has a number of goals in seven discrete areas: housing; employment; social policy; community facilities and environment; economic development; community ownership; and image of the area.

Defining 'partnership'

A review of the literature reveals little common understanding of what precisely is meant by the term partnership. The legal definition of a partnership, in terms of a profit-making business, highlights that all partners are 'jointly and severally liable' for both the successes and failures of the venture. Although this represents a somewhat narrow view, it is a useful starting point as it captures several important facets that characterise a partnership.

It has been suggested that a partnership should seek to achieve an objective that no single organisation could achieve alone – an idea described by Huxham (1993) as 'collaborative advantage'. This is a common concept in business where strategic alliances and joint ventures are only entered into when there is added value to be derived from organisations working collectively. Drawing on the legal definition above, the risks and benefits of the venture need to be shared, so when success is achieved all partners are better off. This implies that there needs to be a degree of mutuality of benefits across partner organisations.

The following is the definition of a cross-sectoral partnership that determined the selection of initiatives to be studied in this report:

> *Three or more organisations – representing the public, private and voluntary sectors – acting together by contributing their diverse resources in the furtherance of a common vision that has clearly defined goals and objectives.*

Expanding upon this definition, the following types of organisations typically enter into partnership initiatives:

- The **public sector** is taken to mean local authorities, regional authorities, central government, quangos, the police, health authorities, and other statutory authorities.

- The **private sector** is taken to mean individual companies, Training and Enterprise Councils (TECs) or Local Enterprise Councils (LECs), Chambers of Commerce, and other representative organisations such as Business in the Community.[2]

- The **voluntary sector** is taken to mean the community and its representatives, self-help groups, voluntary and not-for-profit organisations, and professional organisations such as the Community Volunteer Service (CVS). An important distinction can be made between the community (those people who live and work in an area) and the agencies that represent them. For the sake of brevity, however, the term 'voluntary sector' is used throughout this report to mean both the community and its representatives.

Having now defined what is meant by a partnership in terms of this report, it is important to recognise that there is potential for a gap to exist between the objectives of a partnership initiative on the one hand and what happens in practice on the other.

In an ideal world, the objective of a partnership should be to create an initiative where partners work together to achieve a commonly agreed set of goals and objectives and in so doing deliver more than the sum of its individual components.

In reality, what often happens is that a partnership is simply an initiative existing only as a formal structure that draws together individual interest groups who each use a share of the funds generated by the partnership to 'do their own thing'.

An alternative view was put forward by one of the interviewees who suggested that a partnership can exist on one of three levels.

- First, there is simply agreement in public – partners do not allow differences and disputes to be aired openly and leave each other alone to pursue their own agendas. At this level the partnership exists in name alone, giving the impression of disparate groups operating together.

- Second, partners work within given agendas whilst still retaining an individual perspective on what the initiative ought to be achieving. Whilst such an arrangement might actually deliver tangible outcomes, there is no joint ownership or commitment to a common objective.

- Third, partners work to achieve a commonly agreed set of goals and objectives. At this level, the initiative would be developing the full capacity of all its partners and delivering more than the sum of its individual components.

The key issue that these descriptions allude to is that the term partnership can be used to describe a range of initiatives, only some of which aspire to the model implicit in the definition stated on page 10. The aim of this report is to help those involved in partnerships to achieve an approach to the initiative that is 'working to achieve a commonly agreed set of goals and objectives'.

Why partnership?

The term partnership, and the concepts of multiagency provision and collaboration, have become the buzz words of the 1990s. There are a number of reasons behind this push towards cross-sectoral partnerships as the preferred way of working in addressing a wide range of social, economic and environmental issues.

Firstly, the current political agenda is forcing the pace in this area. Funding requirements for such initiatives as the Single Regeneration Budget (SRB) explicitly require the development of partnerships. The latest *Guide to Bidding for Resources from the Government's Single Regeneration Budget* (1995) says that, for a bid to be successful, it must demonstrate that it includes 'relevant interests in the private and public sectors and in local voluntary and community organisations'.

Secondly, partnerships are often perceived to be the most appropriate vehicle for addressing social and economic needs. Advocates of partnerships argue that, because they offer greater involvement by all sectors of society in the decision-making process, they are seen to be an inherently more efficient way of allocating public funds.

Thirdly, the notion of partnership fits in with the emerging concepts of communitarianism and a stakeholder society. In the recent past there has been a decline in membership of political parties and a concomitant rise in support for local and national pressure groups that tend to deal with a narrow range of social or economic issues. This movement has been accompanied by an increasing desire for more involvement in the provision of local services by people from the local community. In many areas – for example education, health care and crime prevention – people are no longer prepared to sit back and let 'the authorities' dictate what is done, when, and how. Individuals and organisations from all sectors are increasingly demanding a voice in defining and implementing the most appropriate responses to many of the challenges facing society.

Finally, almost all the partnership initiatives included in this report (regardless of the needs they were addressing) recognised that the issues they face are multidimensional. As one interviewee put it:

It is very difficult to look at one aspect of a community – whether it be crime prevention, economic development or improving the environment – without looking at a much wider range of social issues such as housing, transport, health and education.

The point was made, time and again, that most social problems have multiple causes and therefore need a multiagency approach to solutions. This pragmatic push towards partnership initiatives that take on a multifaceted approach throws up four distinct issues.

- Individual partner organisations might only be interested in and qualified to act in a relatively small role. Despite this, they are being asked to sign up to the overall objectives of the partnership.

- In contrast, it is important to recognise that some partners will have a wider agenda than others. Typically, local government, the business sector and TEC/LEC partners will be responsible for a much larger geographical agenda than that prescribed by the confines of a local community-based project.

- A multifaceted approach calls for a concentration of resources and the desire to work towards long-term systemic solutions. However, for a partnership to remain active and vibrant it must also be seen to deliver some short-term successes.

- An initiative that seeks to address a broad range of issues will find there are a large number of agencies outside the partnership that feel they should have an influence over how the initiative evolves.

Each of these four issues are considered in more detail throughout the rest of this report.

Before leaving the issue of why there has been increased interest in partnership initiatives, it should be stressed that many interviewees claimed that this organisational form is not a panacea. A discussion of whether the drive towards devolved partnership arrangements is a good or bad thing is not within the remit of this report. That said, it is legitimate to pose the question to all those who are considering setting up a partnership, is this the most appropriate solution to the issues you are trying to address?

Several interviewees highlighted the need to question why partnerships are set up. As one put it, 'is a cross-sectoral partnership the most effective way of delivering results?' It would seem that the answer to this question might not always be positive. Each of the partnership initiatives included in this report came into existence in different circumstances and for different reasons. Whilst all have been created to deliver tangible benefits to the communities in which they operate, in some instances the form and structure they have adopted might not have been best suited to particular local circumstances.

Deriving common lessons

As has been stated, the purpose of this report is to identify common lessons and examples of good practice from existing initiatives that will be of use to others already working in partnerships or contemplating doing so. In this respect, one of the main findings of the report is that there is a large degree of consensus on what constitutes successful management processes in the development and implementation of partnerships – this, despite the diversity of partnerships studied and the different degrees of success that each initiative has achieved in delivering tangible outputs.

However, the clearest lesson to emerge in this report is that successful partnerships are aware of their context and the impact this has on the way they must operate. Partnerships will exist for different reasons, create different structures, involve different partners and set themselves different goals. This is not an area where 'one size fits all'. There is a wide range of variables – many of them interdependent – which impact upon the choices available to partnerships and which make different

approaches more or less likely to lead to successful outcomes.

The report identifies three such variables, each of which can be thought of as describing a continuum of possible approaches to partnership management. These three variables – the 3 Ps of partnership – are discussed below. The essential point is that one needs to develop a proper understanding of where an initiative lies in respect of these variables in order to be able to decide upon successful approaches to partnership management.

Provenance – how was the partnership established?

The first variable concerns the evolution of the partnership. How and why was the initiative set up? At one end of the spectrum, partnerships can develop naturally out of historical relationships between a number of different agencies working together over time in a particular area.

At another level, it is the common recognition of a particular social, economic or environmental need that is the driving force behind the development of a partnership. In some instances, this occurs as a result of a violent and public manifestation of the need to take action. For example, the TRAX Motor Project in Oxford was established after public disturbances on the Blackbird Leys Estate involving young 'joy-riders'.

In contrast, rather than coming together naturally, or out of a desire to address a particular issue, it is sometimes the case that partners are forced together. For some organisations, involvement in a partnership initiative is a survival mechanism, akin to the process of mergers and take-overs in the business world. Partnerships can offer organisations shared access to power and influence in their local communities, allowing them to achieve something they could not do on their own.

Finally, perhaps the most extreme examples of partnerships that are externally imposed are those that are funding driven – initiatives that draw partners together simply and solely to gain access to public funds. Research by the National Council for Voluntary Organisations on patterns of voluntary sector involvement in the bidding rounds for SRB funding suggests that a large proportion of recently established partnerships fall into this category. This research revealed cases where community or voluntary sector groups were 'involved' in partnership initiatives without being invited to participate in any meaningful way.

Purpose – what are the aims and objectives of the partnership?

Partnerships can set themselves a wide range of different objectives. At one extreme, the goal of a partnership might simply be to represent and lobby on behalf of a particular area or group of people.

At another level, a partnership might confine itself to identifying the needs of a particular area and developing an action plan to meet those needs, without actually putting in place or managing the delivery mechanisms that address those issues it has identified. At this level, the partnership is likely to be advocating existing agencies to take action within a commonly agreed strategic framework. The Sheffield City Liaison Group is an example of a partnership operating in this way.

More frequently, however, a partnership will seek to move beyond these two positions by creating and/or managing the delivery mechanisms that meet the goals it has identified. In simple terms, the initiative moves from *developing* action plans to *implementing* actions. This implies that a partnership will have some control over the physical assets (people, buildings, resources, etc.) that run the projects or provide the services of the initiative. Working at this level, the partnership is likely to remain part of a multiagency approach. Hence, although the partnership has the ability to take action in its own right, it will continue to work with other agencies with which it shares common aims.

Finally, it is possible for a partnership to operate at a fourth level in this continuum. Rather than managing a number of discrete projects, the aim of the partnership might be the long-term delivery of a service, for example a housing management service. This form of partnership implies the need to own and control capital resources and is perhaps best illustrated by the experiences of a community development trust, such as the Shirebrook District Development Trust.

Participation – who is involved in the partnership?

In the same way that partnerships seek to achieve different goals, so they can involve people in a number of different ways. At one level, it might be appropriate simply to keep people *informed* about the work of the initiative – letting people know what the partnership is doing without offering the opportunity to shape or influence the initiative in any way.

At another level, it will be important to *consult* with people who might be affected by the work of the partnership. This process of consultation can take a number of different forms, but the essential element will be that individuals and groups who might not be directly represented by the partnership will have a voice in shaping the initiative. That said, it is important to recognise the potential limitations of any consultation exercise. The whole process will be cosmetic if the important parameters of the initiative (management structures, access to funds, strategic direction, etc.) are not open to debate.

At a third level, involvement in the partnership moves beyond being consulted to actually *participating* in the governance and management of the initiative – that is, being represented in the decision-making processes of the partnership. The efficacy of involvement at this level will depend upon a number of factors, including the intent of the partners, the nature of organisational structure of the initiative, and the ability of partners to participate. However, in theory, participation at this level implies joint control over or access to the 'levers of power'.

Other factors

Having highlighted the '3 Ps of partnership', it is important to recognise that there are several other explanatory variables that determine the critical success factors involved in partnership management. One of the most important, the stage the initiative has reached in its development, is dealt with separately in the next section. Others include:

- the relative power bases of each of the partner organisations

- the funding regime of the partnership – how and where it derives financial support

- the physical, social, economic and political environment in which the partnership operates

- the legal status or constitution of the partnership.

The key issue for those involved in (or contemplating involvement in) a cross-sectoral partnership is to recognise and acknowledge that different initiatives will require different approaches to succeed. As the above discussion has made clear, there are a wide variety of ways in which partnerships come into existence, develop and form.

In many instances, partners and potential partners have little or no control over any of the variables outlined above. The point to remember is that successful outcomes for managing relations within the partnership derive from an understanding and awareness of the background in which the partnership has evolved and developed.

A model of partnership development

Perhaps the most important variable that impacts upon successful partnership management is the stage the initiative has reached in its development. The model set out in Box 2 is intended to give an indication of how a partnership might develop over time.

The model is not meant to be prescriptive – it does not suggest that every partnership must observe each stage of the development process. However, there was a fairly consistent pattern to the development of the partnerships included in this report. The model describes a composite picture drawn from the experience of the initiatives studied. As such, it could be seen to

Box 2 A development model of partnership

Stage 1

- The partners come together through the mutual recognition of a common need, or in a joint effort to obtain public funds.

- If they have not worked together before, the partners begin the process of overcoming differences in backgrounds and approach, building trust and respect.

- There may be a need for training, building each partner's capacity to operate effectively in this new organisation.

Stage 2

- Through a process of dialogue and discussion, the partners establish the common ground and work towards agreeing a vision and mission statement for the initiative.

- The original core group of partners might agree on the need to involve more individuals and organisations in the initiative.

- The partners develop mechanisms for assessing needs and quantifying the size of the task they propose to undertake.

- The initiative combines the information generated by the needs assessment exercise together with the vision and mission statement to produce an agenda for action.

Stage 3

- The formal framework and organisational structure of the partnership is designed and put in place.

- The partners set specific goals, targets and objectives linked into the agenda for action.

- Where appropriate, the executive arm of the partnership selects or appoints a management team (even if this is one person) to oversee the work of the initiative.

Stage 4

- The partnership delivers to its action plan, whether this be service provision or some other function.

- The executive arm seeks to maintain the involvement of all partners, formulates policy decisions and ensures the continuing accountability of the partnership.

- There is an ongoing process of assessing, evaluating and refining the operations of the partnership.

Stage 5

- Where appropriate, the partners should plan their exit strategy. This involves developing a new set of goals for the survival and continuation of the work of the initiative in some form.

- They should seek to create 'life after death' by transferring the assets of the partnership back into the community with which they work.

describe an idealised approach to the development stages that a partnership might aspire to.

In addition, the model is not necessarily sequential – partnership initiatives can move through the stages of development process at a different pace, sometimes attaining goals that are set out in the later stages of development quite early on in their life.

It should also be recognised that the very short time-scales imposed by various funding regimes can cause many partnerships to compress the development process. Inevitably, this may mean that some of the stages of development are missed or only superficially observed. The importance of allowing the partnerships to develop and form over time is considered in greater detail in Chapter 2.

Despite these caveats, the purpose of the model is to provide a framework for examining the critical success factors that impinge upon the partnership management process. The model is used as a guide to lead the reader through the process of partnership development and to highlight the key issues involved in successfully managing cross-sectoral initiatives. The important point for those embarking on this journey is that the partnership development process is not inevitable – it requires time, energy and effort to maintain momentum and drive forward the initiative.

Notes

1 In order to ensure that interviewees spoke frankly about their experiences, we agreed to maintain confidentiality. Hence, the quotes used throughout this report are unattributed.

2 Even at this level of analysis, there is some dispute over the position and role of TECs and LECs. In some partnerships they are seen to represent the private sector, in others they are seen as quangos representing the public sector.

2 The emergence of the partnership

Introduction

In this chapter, we concentrate on the first stage of the development model outlined in Box 2 and examine the initial steps in forming a partnership initiative. Several interviewees drew parallels between partnerships and marriage. People talked about the need for give and take. They stressed the importance of equal treatment, equal respect and equal commitment by all partners. This theme underpins many of the lessons that appear in this chapter.

However, the marriage analogy can only be taken so far. Partnerships operate within a complex context in which a wide range of stakeholders have to be considered. Initiatives claiming community involvement face particular challenges in ensuring representation and accountability.

The following issues were highlighted by interviewees as key to the successful development of a partnership:

- developing relationships – moving from the idea of partnership to a real sense of joint endeavour

- identifying stakeholders – looking beyond the originators of the partnership idea

- selecting partners – deciding who should be involved as partnership members

- representation – exploring the extent to which partnership members are representative of their 'constituencies' and determining the level of involvement different players might have.

Developing relationships

One message was repeated by the vast majority of interviewees – there needs to be an acceptance that a partnership approach will add value to the initiative. This point was reinforced by one who suggested:

> You don't start off with the notion of a partnership for its own sake. You start with a number of interrelated issues and realise that interagency working is the only way to address them.

Allowing time for 'courtship'

A partnership will – by definition – involve bringing together a range of different individuals and organisations, each with their own interests and agendas, to work in new and innovative ways.

Virtually all of the interviewees stressed that in the early stages of the partnership planning process, time has to be built in to allow relationships across the sectors to form properly. Many people extended the analogy between partnerships and marriage to suggest that there is need for a 'courtship' in both relationships. As one person put it:

> If you just pull people round a table and say, 'OK we have got to have a partnership', it won't work. Without a process of courtship it will simply be a shotgun wedding.

Interviewees in those partnerships that had been able to devote time to getting to know one another, to understand each other's aspirations, constraints and agendas, all felt that it had been very worthwhile. For example, one partner from a voluntary organisation said:

for a month, it was basically the four of us locked in a room together and we were having to learn from each other the sort of issues we were each dealing with in our own organisations and the kind of stresses we were under. I think that was quite critical to the process and everybody benefited.

Clearly, the level of pre-existing links will vary from initiative to initiative. Several of the partnerships included in this report grew out of long-standing links across all three sectors. Where this was the case, interviewees recognised and acknowledged how important such links were in speeding up the development process of the partnership.

However, very often the links between the various agencies involved in a partnership initiative are tentative. Indeed, in many cases the individuals and organisations who come together to form the partnership have never met each other before. This is especially true for the voluntary and community sector. Whilst the experience of the partnerships studied suggests that there are often pre-existing links between local authorities and business representatives, these two sectors will traditionally have had fewer opportunities to work collaboratively with voluntary organisations or community groups.

This is an important point because it can make voluntary sector representatives feel at a disadvantage from the outset of the partnership process. Several interviewees from the voluntary sector suggested that during initial discussions they felt they were entering uncharted grounds, whilst for others in the initiative it was familiar territory. As one community representative put it:

I felt I was having to break into a relationship where the other partners already knew the ground rules.

When new links need to be formed, interviewees suggested a range of processes by which this could take place. These include getting people together in consultative meetings, workshops and discussion groups and organising away-days or retreats. At this stage, it was also suggested that it would be beneficial to undertake some type of formal training and development for the individuals involved in the partnership, to enable people to operate more effectively in a new environment. As we shall see in Chapter 4, working in partnership requires a range of skills and competencies that are not necessarily appropriate to other management structures.

KEY LESSONS

However it is achieved, the objective must be to allow people from very different backgrounds the opportunity to learn about:

- each other
- their organisations
- the pressures and constraints under which they operate
- what each can bring to the partnership
- what each hopes to get out of the partnership.

Letting go of prejudices

Time and effort invested at this stage of the development process will pay dividends later. For example, many interviewees suggested that it is more difficult to be in conflict with someone, or to reject their ideas, when you have a proper understanding of *what* they are trying to achieve and *why* they are trying to achieve it. As one interviewee put it:

> *You need to recognise where people are coming from. We can't get rid of our baggage, but you can share it and try to understand other people's baggage.*

Another interviewee described using a facilitated away-day for:

> *bonding and to decide on our rules of engagement – including one which says, if you have a conflict with another member that is nothing to do with the partnership, leave it outside the door. Don't bring it into the boardroom.*

One of the most valuable outcomes from processes designed to increase understanding between partners seems to be a willingness to let go of prejudices in relation to other sectors. Several interviewees said that, if they were honest with themselves, they entered into the partnership initiative fully expecting people from certain sectors to adopt certain positions and to bring or to lack particular skills. For example, interviewees from the private sector frequently mentioned being pleasantly surprised by the level of competency of community representatives. For their part, community sector representatives were relieved to be disabused of the notion that the private sector was simply going to 'parachute in' with inappropriate solutions.

Some of the preconceived notions typically held about each sector are set out in Box 3. The purpose of this analysis is to describe

---

Box 3 Sectoral stereotypes

The public sector

Representatives of local and district authorities (both officers and members) are frequently accused of viewing any move towards working in partnership as a threat. It is suggested that they are not in the habit of having to discuss with anybody what they plan to do in a certain area, other than what is required through statutory consultation procedures.

A successful partnership will be talking to their constituents and empowering them to act; by definition, public sector representatives are no longer in control and could be challenged, questioned and even out-voted.

In addition, a partnership initiative could be seen to be employing people (often on low wages) or using volunteers to carry out activities for which the local authorities are traditionally responsible. Finally, it is possible to view the partnership as competing with the local authority for funds from central government and the European Union.

The private sector

Whilst private sector involvement in partnerships tends to be less politically motivated, representatives from business were also treated with mistrust. The common message was that other partners are nervous about why companies want to become involved – what's in it for them?

Private sector representatives are felt to be far more interested in the overall success of the initiative, rather than in the process by which targets are achieved. This focus means that business representatives can try to take over the initiative – adapting traditional business management techniques to 'solve' the issues as they see them.

In addition, many interviewees claim that business is very conservative. Companies do not like being associated with risk or failure and are only prepared to enter into partnerships that are tackling 'safe, middle-of-the-road' issues.

Finally, the private sector tends to underestimate the skills and abilities of other partners. When things go wrong in the public or voluntary sectors, it is because people are incompetent. When things go wrong in business, management can live with the mistakes because they know they are applying tried and tested techniques and one cannot expect everything to work perfectly all of the time.

The community, their representatives and the voluntary sector

The voluntary sector is seen by many as being obsessed with involving people at the expense of actually making progress towards deliverable targets.

There is also suspicion about what community organisations see themselves in business for. They can be more heavily reliant on the partnership initiative in order to legitimise their own existence. For people in the community and voluntary sector, there are jobs and status at stake. Once a partnership ends, voluntary sector and community representatives will have no role and in some cases no jobs.

The perennial complaint about people from the voluntary sector is that they are unrepresentative – 'they claim to speak for the community, but nobody voted for them'.

the suspicions people often hold about representatives from each sector. It deliberately deals in stereotype, because the stress of working in unfamiliar areas often leads people to behave in ways that are at the extremes of what could be called 'resorting to type'. It is hoped that this somewhat caricatured view of the three sectors will make individuals aware of how they may initially be viewed by others, and demonstrate some of the barriers that need to be broken down if the partnership development process is to be successful.

Balancing development with action

There are, however, two important caveats to be made to the indisputable lesson that relationship building is a process which should not be neglected.

First, there is the practical issue of the constraints imposed by many funding regimes. The SRB bidding process, for example, puts pressure on individuals and organisations to form partnership initiatives within a very short time-frame. Very little can be done to circumvent these pressures, but partners should recognise the potential difficulties that arise from trying to establish a hastily conceived partnership initiative. However, some interviewees said that some of the more significant differences of view only emerged when concrete proposals were on the table. As one put it:

> Within weeks of first getting together, we were having to decide what the priority areas were, what action we wanted to see there, and what it was going to cost. It was great for concentrating the mind and exposing the different angles we were coming from.

The need to move into action quickly can therefore sometimes have its benefits.

Moreover, there will almost inevitably be a tension between the need for a long-term development programme in order to build the roots of the partnership, and the desire for early action and results in order to maintain momentum and enthusiasm. All respondents agreed that a partnership that spends its time talking without achieving anything is likely to fail. Such a process was variously described as 'death by deliberation' and 'consultation fatigue'.

It seems to be helpful, therefore, to think of the development phase as an iterative process; it needs to be handled well enough at the outset in order to build a firm foundation, but is neither an end in itself nor ever really complete.

KEY LESSONS

In summary, the message from those who are already involved in partnerships is clear.

- Make every effort possible to understand the perspective of others involved in the partnership.

- Be open and honest with others so they can understand what it is you are able to bring to the partnership and, equally important, what you are unable to deliver.
- Try to achieve this exchange at the outset, in order to build the foundation for equal treatment, equal respect and equal commitment.
- Finally, however, do not let the process lead to inertia and inaction. In order to secure involvement and support, partners and potential partners need to know that they will be involved in an initiative that has a clear agenda, and a realistic plan of action for meeting that agenda. These issues are discussed in detail in Chapter 3.

Identifying stakeholders

At a very early stage in the development process, those who originally conceived the notion of the partnership will need to decide which individuals and organisations should be involved in the initiative. There can be no universal rules on this matter – much will depend upon what the partnership is trying to achieve and how it aims to fulfil its objectives. Despite this, the experiences of those inter-viewed suggest that there are some general guidelines that need to be observed in selecting partners.

The first stage in deciding which individuals and organisations should become involved in the partnership is to consider who is likely to be affected by the initiative. As we saw in Chapter 1, a partnership can impact upon a wide range of people and will need to involve different groups at a number of different levels.

The term stakeholder best describes those individuals, groups and organisations that will have a legitimate claim to be involved at some level in the work of a partnership.

By definition, the lives and livelihoods of stakeholders will be affected – both positively and negatively – by the initiative. They might expect to benefit from the work of the partnership, or feel threatened by what it hopes to achieve. At the same time, stakeholders are also able to influence the success of the partnership – both positively and negatively – by either supporting it or being hostile to its activities.

One of the biggest challenges in the partnership development process is to identify who are legitimate stakeholders in the work of the initiative. There are several mechanisms by which a partnership can carry out this process. One method is to broadly consider the following four categories.[1]

- **People/organisations who are needed as a resource.** These include potential funders of the partnership; those with experience, expertise and knowledge relevant to the work of the partnership; and those already working in the field addressing issues of importance to the partnership. At later stages it will also include any staff employed by the partnership and other individuals or groups who will deliver the partnership's goals, services or products.

- **People/organisations who will be affected by the initiative**. This might be thought of as the 'client group' of the partnership. It includes the beneficiaries of the partnership and, where appropriate, the users of the service provided by the partnership. It will also include the formal and informal representatives of the 'client group'.

- **People/organisations who are on the sidelines.** These include those groups who might not be directly affected by the work of the partnership, but who live and work in the area where the partnership intends to operate.

- **People/organisations who feel that they have a 'right' to be involved.** There will be certain individuals or groups which the partnership will have to involve simply because they need their backing. As supporters of the partnership, their role might be little more than a figure-head; but if they were to be excluded they could represent formidable opponents to the initiative.

Categorising stakeholders in this way will help to establish which individuals and organisations are critical to the progress and success of the partnership development process. Another method of mapping stakeholders is shown in Figure 1, which is drawn from the work of Johnson and Scholes (1993). Here, the

Figure 1 Stakeholder mapping: power/interest matrix

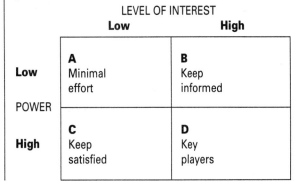

	LEVEL OF INTEREST	
	Low	High
Low	**A** Minimal effort	**B** Keep informed
POWER		
High	**C** Keep satisfied	**D** Key players

power and interest level of different stakeholders is assessed, enabling partners to determine what levels of activity are appropriate for keeping such stakeholders 'on board'.

By classifying stakeholders in relation to the power they hold and the extent to which they are likely to show an interest in the activities of the partnership, an initiative is better able to decide the type of relationship that needs to be formed with each stakeholder group. This issue is returned to in the section on representation (page 27).

An alternative but complementary approach to this process of stakeholder mapping is described by Obeng and Crainer (1994). This involves asking a series of questions about the proposed activities of the partnership. Figure 2 presents an interpretation of this stakeholder map for use by partnership initiatives.

What this stakeholder map attempts to underline is that the work of a partnership can impact across a wide range of individuals and organisations. It is not simply enough to consider those groups which the partnership seeks to 'help'. There will be many more influential parties who have the potential to 'make or break' the development of an initiative.

Inevitably, there will be individuals or organisations which mistrust the motives of any project. Such people are often able to delay or block the potential success of the partnership. One interviewee representing the private sector recalled the early days of the initiative and the frustrations caused by mistrust.

There was a lot of resistance in the early days and suspicion of the private sector getting involved at all, because we hadn't previously. Once public sector agencies were involved, the local people saw us as such a concentration of outsiders – though community agencies were in there too – they began to resent what they saw as a parachute initiative with a bunch of civil servants and businessmen deciding where the money went. They formed a steering group, ostensibly to help channel the money, but in practical terms it was acting as a block and not much was getting invested. The community got frustrated, the steering group got frustrated, and those of us representing companies got frustrated.

This experience led to a recognition amongst

Figure 2 A stakeholder map

Stakeholders	Public sector	Private sector	Voluntary sector
Who wants the partnership to succeed? Who would like to see the partnership fail? Who is offering the partnership support? Whose support is necessary for the partnership to succeed? Who is offering the partnership resources (time, money, expertise, knowledge)? Whose success does the partnership affect? Whose success affects the partnership? Who will benefit from the work of the partnership? Who might be damaged by the work of the partnership?			

the private sector representatives involved that the initiative would only succeed if it was genuinely community led, and eventually a board was formed in which the majority of the directors were from the local population.

The general lesson appears to be that there might be certain groups who feel alienated by the work of the partnership. Founding partners need to aware of this and try to manage relations with them so that, even if they do not become part of the partnership, at least they are dissuaded from sabotaging its efforts.

KEY LESSONS

A vital stage in the partnership development process is to identify different stakeholder groups and take appropriate action to ensure they do not feel alienated or threatened.

Very often, partnership proposals are seen to be 'wrong' or 'inappropriate', not because they are inherently unsound but because key influencers have not been involved in the formulation process.

Selecting partners

Whilst a vast range of groups may have a stake in the outcomes of a partnership's work, formal membership of the partnership must, for reasons of practicality, be limited. Choices will therefore have to be made as to who exactly is to be involved.

Individuals or organisations?
When talking about the composition of the partnership, especially in relation to involvement at the executive level, several interviewees felt that choosing the right individual to become involved is sometimes more important than having a specific organisation on board. As one interviewee said:

Partnerships start with individuals, not organisations.

In another case, the chair of a partnership was quite explicit in saying that she selected fellow board members on the basis of their skills and abilities to get the job done.

Once I had been in [the area] for 18 months, I knew who the movers and shakers were and, equally, the people who were willing to work. I went and talked to them and said 'These are the particular skills I want you to bring along – can you do that?'

Many interviewees stressed the importance of attracting people who command a degree of power within their organisations. It was suggested that the work of a partnership can be slowed down considerably if individual representatives do not have the authority to sanction specific proposals and actions put forward by the partnership. Individual members of the partnership need to know how their own organisation works and be able to command the resources of that organisation. In essence, they need to be able to carry the commitment of their organisation in a single voice. In one of the partnerships studied, the local authority was initially represented by a very junior officer, with, as one of the private sector members recalled, serious consequences for the early credibility of the partnership.

We were very naïve at the outset. The local people were brassed off, to put it mildly, with the council. They told us nothing had been done for years, no one listened to them, etc., etc. We took them at face value, and the guy from the council didn't put us wise. Of course, once we made

25

contact with councillors and senior officers, they didn't take too kindly to us basically saying 'we'll succeed where you've failed'. It was only once we got [current local authority representative] and she guided us through the internal politics and explained the sensitivities and the efforts that had been made in the area that we were able to start building bridges.

In addition, by making an initial contact with a senior and influential person within an organisation, the partnership will have access to a large network which can be used to lever in other people and resources to help develop the initiative. In simple terms, gaining the support and backing of one or two powerful or influential people at the beginning of the partnership development process makes it easier to attract others.

An exception to this rule was mentioned in one partnership. In this case, organisations from the three sectors were pulled together very quickly to meet an SRB bid deadline. The time pressures meant that the bulk of the work was done by middle-ranking representatives. One of those involved in that early stage of work said:

When we put the initial SRB group together it was very fortuitous that the people involved were capable of stepping outside their organisations, maybe because they weren't at a terribly senior level. They didn't have that vested interest. Once people at Chief Executive level got involved, it became more complex because they had much more stake in 'what does this mean for my organisation and for me?'

Building organisational links

Whatever their level, reliance on building strong links with individuals does have the potential

problem that people leave organisations and move on. To combat this, members of the partnership should think about succession planning. One interviewee suggested:

The key is to use one individual to 'make friends' with other people in the organisation they represent – get to know people and make links. Knowledge about the work of the partnership cascades and there is someone there to take up the role if your original member moves on.

Coping with 'passengers'

Whilst targeting potential 'star' members might be the most efficient way of operating, it is clear that not all partners will be involved because they have the relevant experience and knowledge. As was noted above, it is sometimes the case that individuals and organisations feel they should be involved in a partnership by 'right'. Very little can be done about this and it often falls to the chair of the partnership to manage the relations at the executive level to get the best out of all the partners involved. This was summed up by one person who said:

There is a point where you have to say, 'oh well, so and so is on the board despite the fact they contribute nothing'. It is almost a matter of duty. You just have to get on with it.

KEY LESSONS

Where there is choice about who joins the partnership, look for individuals who have the skills and a willingness to contribute, but see them as a gateway into their organisation. Be prepared to include people whose potential contribution is less obvious in order to keep the peace or access vital resources.

Representation

One of the major concerns expressed by all the interviewees was a desire to ensure that the legitimacy of the partnership is established and maintained within a particular community. A necessary (but not sufficient) condition in this respect is that the members of the partnership are representative of the groups they claim to speak for.

The issue of representation was frequently felt to be more important when applied to those in the community and voluntary sector. Very few people questioned, for example, whether a senior executive of a TEC or Chamber of Commerce could legitimately speak for the business community. There often appeared to be an unspoken assumption that both the private sector and public sector are somehow homogeneous groups and representatives for each are able to speak with one voice. This is clearly a myth. It is important to recognise the diversity of each of the sectors involved in a partnership and to question how far representatives from each sector are able to speak for a broader community.

In contrast to attitudes held about public and private sector representatives, attitudes towards the voluntary and community sector were far more questioning. Community representatives, for example, were often accused by people from the private and statutory sectors of being nothing more than local activists. As one interviewee (who is a member of a partnership management team charged with implementing policies) put it:

How can community representatives be said to speak for anyone other than a minority of well-intentioned but vocal and skilled individuals who might represent particular interest groups rather than the wider community?

Another interviewee from the business sector expressed a more pragmatic viewpoint:

I think it is false to think of community 'reps' as being representative and accountable in the way that local authority members might claim. It is a simple fact of life that those local 'reps' who are elected to serve as board members are acknowledged within the community to have their heads screwed on. Not everyone in the community will agree with their views, but they are there because they have earned their stripes, have been active players, and are willing to commit their time.

The issue that appears to lie at the heart of this question of representation is the tension between activism and apathy. Whilst a partnership initiative might seek to be truly representative of the community in which it operates, not all members of that community will want to be involved or even represented. This point was best described by one interviewee in the following terms:

Because a partnership is active in an area, there is an expectation that it must have the full understanding, knowledge and backing of all the residents in the community. That doesn't happen and never will happen – 90 per cent of any population simply don't want to know. Somebody tells them what is happening and they say 'well fine, get on with it, but please don't ask me to come along to a meeting because I prefer to spend my evenings watching TV'. That is their right.

This view was further developed by another interviewee who questioned the emphasis that is placed on this need for the representation and involvement of the local community:

> *If one looks at local or national government, how many people understand, know about and support their activities? Does that reduce the legitimacy of government? Do not apply rules or expectations to local community-based projects that are not applied in other circumstances.*

In this context, the important issue would appear to be the structures and processes by which potential representatives are selected. As such, it is perhaps ironic that community representatives can, in certain circumstances, be considered the most democratic and accountable of all actors who enter into a partnership. In one partnership, for example, to be a community board member the individual has to be involved on one of a number of neighbourhood councils. Each year these councils hold an annual general meeting to which every resident is invited and has a right to vote. Several other partnerships also hold annual elections for community board members; these are open to anyone who lives in the area, whether or not they have a previous track record in community involvement.

As with so many other aspects of partnership, many interviewees mentioned the need for balance. Initiatives that do not engage and involve members of the community in which they operate run the risk of failure – it is natural for people to feel suspicious of, and hostile towards, an initiative that is trying to change things in a particular area without any reference to the people living and working in that area.

But, as we saw earlier, partnerships which spend all their time talking without taking action are also doomed to failure. Several interviewees expressed the fear that, in seeking to be representative, a partnership runs the risk of degenerating into a talking shop. As one person put it:

> *If you spend ages trying to develop from the base, it won't work, the momentum isn't there. You need something to show, something in the shop window, before people will be attracted to become involved. Local people, by and large, aren't interested in the process, they're interested in the outputs.*

Participation

The key lesson for success in this area is not simply to identify those who are the stakeholders in a partnership, but also to ensure they have access to information, consultative procedures and decision-making powers. Perhaps one of the most influential texts on participation in partnership initiatives was that written in 1969 by Sherry Arnstein, a former Chief Advisor to the US Government. She developed a 'Ladder of Citizen Participation' that provided a typology of eight different levels of power and involvement citizens might have in government initiatives. More recently, this model has been adapted by Wilcox (1994a) who describes 'five stances of participation'. These comprise:

- information – tell people what is planned

- consultation – offer a number of options and listen to the feedback

- deciding together – encourage others to provide additional ideas and options and join in deciding the best way forward

- acting together – not only do different interests decide together what is best, but they form a partnership to carry it out

- supporting independent community interests – help others do what they want; perhaps within a framework of grants, advice and support provided by the resource holder.

Wilcox elaborates these five stances of participation and puts forward the processes and methods by which different groups can be involved at each level of the partnership management process. The key issue that this model highlights (and one that is strongly reinforced by the experiences of those involved in this research study) is that successful partnership management depends upon attaining the *appropriate* level of involvement for all its stakeholders.

The preceding discussion has tried to demonstrate that there will be limits upon the degree to which representatives of each of the three sectors either wish to, expect to, or are able to become involved in the work of the partnership. Put simply, it is legitimate for partnerships to involve different stakeholder groups at different levels in the management processes, from receiving information, through consultation, to participation in decision-making.

This said, it is important to recognise two issues. Firstly, it is not only significant at

what *level* stakeholders are involved in the management process, the *time* at which they are invited to participate in the development of the partnership can also be of great importance. Those involved in the initial stages will have greater potential to influence the scope and direction of the partnership initiative.

Secondly, access to the decision-making process will depend critically upon the governance, management and organisational structure of the partnership initiative. These issues are dealt with in detail in Chapter 4.

KEY LESSONS

The greatest fallacy in partnership management is to assume that 'everyone must have a voice'. A partnership needs to develop a clear understanding of who is legitimately able to participate in the work of the initiative. This understanding can only be derived from a formal exercise that both *identifies* the stakeholders in a partnership and *assesses* the degree to which each is able to contribute to the work of the initiative.

Note

1 This approach has been adapted from Obeng and Crainer's work on business process re-engineering, *Making Reengineering Happen* (Pitman, 1994).

3 Developing a vision and mission

Introduction

There was almost unanimous agreement amongst our interviewees that a shared vision is vital for a partnership to succeed. When asked to name the two or three critical success factors that a partnership has to get right, over half the people we spoke to cited some variation on a 'common vision'.

Whilst this may appear to be plain common sense, it is something that is easy to say but harder to achieve. Moreover, vision alone does not bring about the sort of change that most partnerships are seeking. It needs to be harnessed and allied to more prosaic processes, including objective setting, planning and monitoring.

In this chapter, we explore the second stage in the development cycle – the processes by which partnerships agree their *raisons d'être* and the means by which they are to be achieved. Whilst the terms 'vision' and 'mission' were not used by all of the partnerships studied for this report, they were in common enough usage for us to adopt them here as generic labels.

Vision and mission

The two concepts are closely interrelated and often the terms are interchanged. Whilst this can lead to some confusion, in practice the distinction between the two elements is straight-forward. It may be useful for us to distinguish at the outset what we mean by the two terms.

Vision is an intellectual expression of the rationale of the partnership. It indicates why the partnership exists and often describes an inspiring purpose that unifies the interests of all the partners. It may or may not be written down, but it is generally short and capable of being memorised.

The **mission** of an organisation does tend to be written down, as it is often one of the means by which the body seeks to hold itself to account with its client groups. The mission statement usually describes the ways in which the partnership will ensure the practical application of its vision. Often, as in the example set out in Box 5 opposite, the mission is written in terms of a series of aims and objectives for the partnership.

Box 4 Partnership visions

The Netherton Partnership
'To create a sustainable regeneration process, unlocking Netherton's full potential and making the area vibrant, attractive and prosperous where people want to live, work and play and businesses choose to invest and develop.'

The TRAX Motor Project
'To channel the natural enthusiasm of young people for vehicles into a positive and challenging direction, to aid their development towards further achievement.'

> **Box 5 A partnership mission**
>
> **The Ebor Gardens Partnership – aims and objectives**
> - To promote and support new and existing initiatives to improve the self-esteem of the residents.
> - To identify and encourage resources from all areas of the community to play an active role in fulfilling the vision.
> - To develop a better understanding of challenges facing the residents of the estate and the initiatives already in place, and how these are impacting on daily lives.
> - To make available the appropriate skills and resources which enable residents to achieve their maximum personal potential to lead fulfilled lives.
> - To ensure a consistent communication framework is established to inform and consult all residents of the initiatives taking place on the estates.

In summary, vision describes *what* the partnership aims to achieve. The mission statement explains more *how* the partnership seeks to operate.

Developing vision

The way in which a vision will be developed seems, in some measure, to be a function of the *provenance* of the partnership. Where formation of a partnership is prompted by some kind of crisis or severe problem, the vision may be almost self-evident. One of the founder members of the TRAX Motor Project spoke of 'an obvious problem which concentrated everyone's minds and forced a solution'.

Where partners are forced together, to seek SRB funding, for instance, or to secure their futures, agreeing on a common vision seems to be more difficult. On the surface, there is often a clear and shared view of what the partnership should aim to achieve, but this sometimes proves to be skin-deep. In one partnership, many private sector organisations were drawn together following a Business in the Community 'Seeing is Believing' visit. They found community groups interested in partnership working and quite quickly organised themselves around a seemingly shared vision of improving people's prospects and quality of life. However, once the partnership tried to move forwards into consultation and action planning, it became apparent that some members saw the partnership as having an enabling role – supporting the community in lobbying, securing resources and so on – whilst others expected it to be more directly involved, for instance by providing job placement opportunities and training.

Once again, the lesson that emerges from the partnerships studied is that the development of shared vision is a process that needs time, and in which partners should be prepared to be open with one another about what they can contribute, the constraints they face and their own expectations of the partnership and of one another.

Before leaving this issue of the importance of

vision to the partnership development process, it is worth mentioning a related topic that was raised by several of the interviewees. This concerns the existence, in some partnerships, of an individual who is seen as the 'visionary force' driving the development of the partnership.

Such individuals derive power and influence from their ability to articulate their ideas and encourage others to 'buy into the project'. If they have developed other partnerships in the past, or seen similar solutions work in other circumstances, then they are better able to do this. They have the talent to create a common recognition that something needs to be done, and to get partners to negotiate and mediate an agreement on objectives.

Although several of the interviewees could identify with this role of 'visionary' or 'charismatic leader', it is not something that is found in all partnership initiatives. Where such individuals do exist, however, it is important to stress that they might come from any sector – they might be a community entrepreneur, a senior private sector leader, or an influential politician.

The point that interviewees were keen to stress is that a 'visionary' figure can play a pivotal role in the establishment and development of the partnership. Whilst not necessarily the best person to lead the initiative once it is established, he/she can contribute a great deal in the early stages.

Occasionally where a visionary leader is the driving force behind a partnership's formation, the process of developing a vision can serve a slightly different purpose. Where people follow a visionary because they are attracted by his/ her charisma, there is a risk that they end up supporting what is essentially an entrepreneurial operation; developing a truly *shared* vision minimises this risk.

KEY LESSONS

Where an initiative does have a powerful advocate or charismatic leader, make use of this person's energy, enthusiasm and ability to inspire others in the creation of a common vision for the partnership.

The acid test for a vision seems to be whether or not it provides an enduring reference point for the partnership – is it something on which the members can reflect when difficult issues have to be resolved, and does it inform decision-making or simply lead to more debate?

Developing a mission statement

There are a large number of management texts that can help an organisation both define and refine its mission statement.[1] In the following paragraphs, we aim to highlight the key issues that may affect partnerships that seek to develop a mission statement.

The list of questions set out in Box 6 offers a checklist to help those involved in a partnership think more clearly about the issues that should be addressed in a mission statement. In trying to adapt this framework for the likely audiences of this report, we have been struck by an issue which many interviewees raised – language. Every section of society tends to develop its own 'jargon', and words and phrases used in one sphere may have a completely different meaning when used in another. Paying attention to language, ensuring that words are taken to mean the same thing by all those

Box 6 A checklist for developing a mission statement[2]

Purpose
- Why does the partnership exist?
- What does the partnership hope to achieve?
- What is the inspiring purpose that unifies the interests of all the partners?

Strategy
- In which area will the partnership operate? (This might be a geographical area; serving the needs of a particular social group; or dealing with a specific issue.)
- What are the strategic goals of the initiative – the few key things it really needs to achieve to make its vision real?

Values
- What values and principles underpin the work of the partnership – what are the 'non-negotiables' about the way the partnership wishes to work?
- Are all the partners able to 'sign up' to these values?
- Do these values match the partnership's strategy – will the aspirations for ways of working support the work of the partnership, or hinder it?

Structure and resources
- What is the governance and management structure of the partnership – how are decisions about direction made, and by whom, and how is the partnership run on a day-to-day basis?
- What resources are (or will be) committed to the aims and objectives of the partnership?

Action
- How will the partnership achieve its purpose?
- Who will be responsible for delivering the agenda of the partnership?
- What are the mechanisms by which the outputs and outcomes of the partnership will be judged?

present, is time-consuming, but seems to be important not just to avoid misunderstandings but also to bond the partners together and build a sense of equality. One community representative in a partnership dominated by the private sector, explained her early feelings of exclusion as follows:

It was just awful at the beginning. All these business people spouting initials and words I'd never heard of. It took a lot of courage, but eventually I had to jump in and say that they were leaving me behind. That made them slow down and think about what they were saying. To be honest with you, I think some of them were thinking the same thing, but nobody wanted to be the one who looked stupid.

By focusing on processes, as well as on resource inputs, the development of a mission statement can further emphasise equality between partners. As one founder member of a partnership put it:

Partnerships will only succeed if all views carry equal weight. But it is inevitable that status will be reflected by the amount of money or gifts that an organisation can put up, which means the voluntary sector is always down the pecking order. The only answer is to formalise equality through the early development process by addressing issues such as values and decision-making processes.

KEY LESSONS

A mission statement should:
- bring together all the partners around an agreed set of aspirations
- provide a framework which describes the activities the partnership seeks to undertake (and by implication indicates which activities are excluded)
- outline the specific targets and goals of the partnership
- specify the processes and procedures by which these targets and goals will be achieved
- describe what resources the partnership will utilise.

Understanding the issues

In trying to answer the questions laid out in Box 6, it is evident that the creation of a partnership mission statement cannot take place in a vacuum. As with any planning process, in order to draw up a mission statement, it is necessary to have an understanding of the area in which the initiative intends to operate. Such an understanding can only be properly derived from a formal process of data gathering that considers a wide range of indices that measure the human and economic capital of an area. As one interviewee put it:

You need a fundamental study of the physical, the economic, the environmental and the other problems of a particular area. If you like, what its pathology is, what its opportunities are, what its difficulties are, and what its relationship is with other areas.

Clearly, the precise details of how to conduct such an exercise will be dependent upon what the partnership is trying to achieve, for whom, and in which areas. There can be no 'off-the-shelf' method to understanding the environment and culture in which the partnership intends to operate. Bearing this in mind, this section attempts to indicate some broad, generic approaches to conducting the type of analysis that is needed to underpin the development of a partnership's mission statement.

Virtually every partnership included in this report went through a formal process of data gathering. These were variously described as a 'mapping exercise', a 'needs analysis' or a 'baseline study'.

Despite this potential for diversity, set out in Box 7 are three different, but complementary,

Box 7 Informing the partnership

1 Analyse published data

There is a mass of freely available statistical data on a wide range of social and economic indices. These include information on health, housing conditions, educational provision and attainment, unemployment, job prospects, opportunities for leisure pursuits, crime and policing, the take-up of benefit, land use and economic activity.

Much of this information is collated at a national, regional and local level. Many of the organisations entering a partnership initiative will have a legal or statutory duty to collect such information. Potential sources include the planning and economic development departments of local and district authorities; TECs and LECs; voluntary sector agencies; health authorities; and local universities and colleges which often conduct research into these issues.

In interpreting published data, one should attempt to not just look at the bald statistics but infer the needs implied by them. In addition, it is important to consider the future – what are the prevailing trends in social and economic conditions; what potential developments are known about; how might these affect the issues under consideration?

2 Analyse existing provision

Beyond considering background information about a given area or issue, it is worthwhile examining what other organisations might be doing to address similar or related issues to those identified by the partnership. The purpose of such an exercise is to establish what needs are currently being addressed and identify any gaps in provision.

Perhaps one of the most difficult tasks in such an exercise is identifying the organisations to approach. It is important to try and canvass the views of small community groups as well as the more prominent voluntary organisations. Research amongst these organisations can be conducted by postal questionnaire, telephone interviews or face-to-face discussions.

3 Ask the 'target audience'

Finally, it is clear that the most direct and relevant information will be obtained from those individuals with whom the partnership seeks to work. This might be the residents of a local area, a particular group such as young offenders, or a broader community such as working mothers.

Whatever the size of the 'total population', conducting a meaningful research exercise amongst a sample need not be prohibitively time-consuming or expensive. Many of the partnerships studied have either conducted such research themselves or commissioned other organisations to carry it out for them.

methods of collecting and collating data in order to form a better understanding of those issues that a partnership might seek to address. Whilst these three approaches are drawn largely from the experience of partnerships working in areas of environmental, economic or social regeneration, it is easy to see how they can be adapted to a wide range of different initiatives.

Some of the partnerships had used resources such as local universities to help them in the data-gathering process, and this is a useful way of building further links with another sector. Where expert help seems to be most useful is in interpreting the data collected. Statistics can often appear contradictory – due to differences in collection methods or timing – and the categorisations used by many research bodies may not fit easily with the layperson's understanding of society. There is often a need for a focused analysis of published data by someone experienced in judging the 'quality' of the information available.

Another caveat that emerges from the experience of some of the partnerships we studied is the need for management of expectations when seeking data from the 'target audience'. Particularly when large numbers of high-profile private sector organisations are involved in a partnership, local people may expect to see high levels of inputs. The experience of at least one of the case study partnerships suggests that care needs to be taken to ensure that local consultation on needs does not simply result in the production of an overambitious 'wish list', the corollary to which is likely to be cynicism and distrust.

Clearly, a data-gathering exercise is only the first step in this process. The next and, for many partnerships we studied, more problematic

stage, is to prioritise the issues into a coherent strategy for action. There is clearly much scope for dispute and conflict when trying to decide what a partnership should do. As one respondent from a partnership dealing with issues of economic regeneration put it:

> *You ask anyone in this area what they want – new windows, central heating or jobs? Do they want nice flowers in the streets, improved lighting or jobs? That is what it is all about, they want jobs. They want to be able to choose their own lifestyle and be free from a dependency on benefits.*

The nature of this conflict returns us to the issues raised in Chapter 2 about the balance between long-term and short-term goals in the development of a partnership. In this instance, the community sees the creation of job opportunities as the appropriate solution to the problems they face. The question this particular partnership had to resolve was how much effort should be put into short-term improvements in the physical environment whilst striving towards increasing employment prospects in the long-term.

This dichotomy between the long- and short-term can produce further tensions in a partnership initiative. One might take the long-term view that the work of a partnership initiative is to serve not simply the existing community but a future one. If part of what the partnership is aiming to do is, for example, to conduct a programme of economic and social regeneration, then the existing community in a given area will have a different set of issues from the potential future community.

It is not possible to provide simple solutions to the problems raised in this process of issue analysis and strategy development. The clear lesson to emerge from those partnerships studied was that there is a paramount need to involve not only all the partners but as wide an audience as possible in defining and prioritising the issues. This need for involvement and participation is the golden thread that binds together successful partnerships. It is an issue that is returned to in Chapter 4.

KEY LESSONS

In order to develop its vision and mission, a partnership needs to generate a common understanding of the issues it seeks to address and the scope of activity the initiative aims to undertake. These processes of analysis and strategy development go hand in hand. For each to be meaningful, however, they must involve all of the partners who must have a say in:

- how issues are identified
- how these issues are prioritised
- how actions and objectives are decided upon.

Development is a process not an activity

Before turning to the next stages of the partnership development process, it is important to stress that the work of partnership formation never stops. For each of the issues considered thus far there is a continual need to review and update.

Several interviewees stressed that the preparation that takes place in the initial stages of the partnership formation is an endless task. There will always be scope for further developing relations, creating a greater understanding between the partners, and learning how to maximise the potential of working together. In addition, as the partnership develops, new

individuals and organisations will become involved. Several of the initiatives studied recognised this and had developed formal induction programmes for new people as they entered the partnership.

The vision and mission of the partnership will also need to be revisited from time to time in order to ensure that the work of the initiative still accords with the original intentions. If there is some tension between what was envisioned for the partnership and what is actually taking place, then there is a need for review of the situation.

On the one hand, it might be that the activities the partnership is now undertaking have, for whatever reasons, strayed from the planned strategy. Alternatively, it might be the case that, over time, the vision and mission of the partnership have become inappropriate because external circumstances have changed. Further, a review of the work of the partnership might highlight issues and areas that are not being addressed, despite being targeted in the original vision and mission.

Such tensions and gaps will require a rethinking of the aims and objectives of the partnership and will involve returning to the initial stages of the partnership development process. There will be a need to ask such fundamental questions as:

- have we still got the right people involved?

- is a partnership still the right structure for achieving our aims?

- is this still a worthwhile initiative that merits continued support and development?

Finally, it will also be necessary to monitor the external environment continually and to ensure that the partnership is meeting the needs of the people it aims to help and support. Hence, the kind of mapping exercise described in Box 7 should be part of a regular review process, rather than simply a one-off initial assessment.

KEY LESSONS

The importance of developing a vision and mission statement for a partnership cannot be overstressed. Not only do they help to shape the development of the initiative in the early stages, but they provide a constant reminder to everyone (both inside and outside the partnership) of the aims and objectives of the partnership.

The process of developing clarity and commonality in vision and mission requires time and a commitment to be open from all partners. It needs to be informed by data from the field in which the partnership seeks to operate. Investment in these areas in the early stages of partnership formation pays off in the long run in terms of:

- better working relations, both within the partnership and between the partnership and the community outside
- more effective decision-making.

Notes

1 See, for example, *Do You Have a Mission Statement?* by A. Campbell and S. Yeung (Economist Publications, 1990).

2 Developed from Andrew Campbell's work in *Mission and Business Philosophy* (A. Campbell and K. Tawadey, Butterworth-Heinemann, 1990).

4 Governance, management and decision-making

Introduction

Most of the partnerships included in this report had, at an early point in their development process, established a formal constitution or legal structure. Generally, this structure provides the framework for decision-making processes and defines the roles and responsibilities of those involved in the governance and management of the partnership.

This said, even amongst the 12 partnerships studied, there was a wide variety of structures and organisational forms. There are a number of organisations that can provide advice on the relative merits of different types of constitutions.[1] This report, therefore, does not seek to provide guidance in this area, beyond recognising the various forms a partnership might take. Represented amongst the case study partnerships were the following:

- an unincorporated association where the partnership does not have a separate legal existence (it is worth noting that such an apparently loose form does not necessarily imply small-scale operations; one such partnership we studied was involved in over 80 projects, with a budget in excess of £50 million)

- an association incorporated as a separate legal entity

- a company limited by guarantee, whose constitution will be prescribed by its memorandum and articles of association

- other formal structures such as a community development trust, which usually takes the form of a limited company, but will by definition remain a non-profit-making organisation.

A partnership that adopts any of these various structures might also feel it appropriate to apply for charitable status.

Rather than concentrate on the narrow issue of the legal constitution of a partnership initiative, this chapter looks in greater detail at the governance and management structures a partnership might choose to put in place. Whilst partnership structures can vary considerably, the results of this research suggest that the most common organisational structure is one that comprises three discrete elements:

- a governance function – the executive body of the partnership

- a management function – those who are charged with implementing the partnership's activities

- a consultative function – the various committees, subcommittees and steering groups that report to the executive body.

It is important to recognise that there are no formal definitions, nor commonly agreed usage, for any or each of these terms. For example, in some partnerships the governance function is carried out by an 'executive board' or a 'management committee'. In others, the management function resides with a group known as the 'executive team' or the 'resource team'.

This simple description of the typical organisational structure of a partnership throws up some important issues about clarifying where the real power and authority of the initiative lies. The following sections consider the role of each part of the partnership structure; the relationships that need to be formed across them; and how the organisational structure will impact upon the decision-making processes of the initiative.

The role of the board

Typically, the role of the partnership board (the executive body of the partnership) is to set the parameters for the initiative. For those involved in the initial stages of development, this function will include defining and developing the vision and mission of the partnership.

Once established, the board is likely to concentrate on such tasks as policy formulation and the accountability of the partnership, and will be asked to determine, approve and endorse key areas and activities to ensure that the strategic direction of the initiative is maintained. To fulfil these functions, the board will have reported to it the progress and performance of all aspects of the partnership's work at regular intervals. Other than in very small and focused partnerships, the purpose of such reports will be to enable the board to carry out its governance role, rather than to allow management supervision.

Further into the development cycle, the board will become involved in planning the long-term development of the partnership. In many instances (especially for those initiatives that are time-limited by a specific funding regime) this will involve planning a suitable exit strategy to ensure that the work of the initiative endures after the partnership itself ceases to exist.

The size of the board

As the preceding description implies, the board can be seen as the 'heart and soul' of the partnership. As such, it is easy to see why all stakeholders would seek to be represented at this level of the partnership's activities. However, as interviewees from all three sectors made clear, it is simply impractical to attempt to include too many representatives at the partnership board level. To do so risks causing the initiative to degenerate into a 'talking shop', with many voices being heard but no clear direction emerging or decisions being taken.

Whilst it would be wrong to be over-prescriptive, experience of the partnerships studied suggests that between 10 and 14 representatives at the board level is somewhere near the optimal number.

These observations were mirrored in the recent Report of the Commission on the Future of the Voluntary Sector (1996), which suggested that:

> *large boards are generally ineffective. Once numbers rise much above 12–15, discussion and debate becomes difficult.*

Although the findings of the Commission are specifically related to voluntary sector organisations, there are strong parallels with the governance structure of partnerships.

KEY LESSONS

Virtually all the interviewees involved in the partnerships studied endorsed the view that any organisation can only function efficiently and effectively if executive power lies with a relatively small team of representatives. Attempts to create unwieldy bureaucracies that allow every interest group (no matter how peripheral) to influence the decision-making process are unworkable.

Representation on the board

Whilst membership of the partnership board needs to be restricted, interviewees were keen to stress the importance of finding a balanced composition of board members. By definition, membership of the partnership board confers access to power and influence over the activities of the initiative. As such, it is vital that the membership of the board is representative of the stakeholders in the initiative.

The key issue in this respect is equality. Amongst interviewees, there was consensus around the pragmatic view that in most partnerships it is unlikely that all parties will have equivalent power. Indeed, it was often stressed that one of the essential features of a partnership is the explicit recognition that each partner brings distinct strengths to the relationship. Many interviewees said that, for a partnership to function, there must be a willingness to make creative use of what is on offer from each partner in terms of money, time, expertise, knowledge, energy, etc.

Despite these good intentions, it was clear to everyone interviewed for this report that money and political authority remain the traditional 'levers of power'. There is always a danger that, despite the rhetoric of partnership, those with access to money and political clout are able to control the decision-making process. Perhaps not surprisingly, this fear is expressed most frequently by representatives from community groups and the voluntary sector.

Looking at the partnership initiatives involved in this study, two specific strategies emerge for dealing with this issue. The first concerns the composition of the board. One partnership studied, for example, had a board of fifteen made up of eight community representatives, four from the private sector, two from local government and one observer from central government. One board member described this situation as:

> the voting power being in inverse proportion to the hard cash and other resources that people could bring to the table.

It was explicitly recognised by all partners that the underlying principle was that the community had an absolute majority and that decisions could not be 'forced through' against the wishes of the community.

In this example, if the local council wanted to propose some new development, it could be blocked by the community representatives at the board. On the other hand, if the community representatives argued for a certain project, they could actually force a vote through and adopt this as policy, but other partners still controlled the 'purse strings'. The resources would not automatically feed through to implement the policy of the partnership. As another board member of this partnership commented:

> I think it was well structured to require it to work. It forced the partners to be honest and open, to work with and persuade others, and agree what are the priorities. Otherwise, either the thing wouldn't happen or resources wouldn't flow properly to support the objectives of the partnership.

The second strategy for ensuring equality is for the partnership board to proceed by consensus. In several partnerships, the board had explicitly adopted a non-voting system – every partner has to agree to decisions or effectively there is a veto. One councillor who is a member of a rather large partnership board felt there was no alternative to the consensus model:

The point of this system is we never lose. Are never seen to lose – that's the important thing from the political viewpoint. People shift their position, but no one ever actually loses. We're adversarial enough as it is – if there was a voting structure it would be chaos.

In such instances, community and voluntary sector representatives felt that (in crude terms), despite the fact that the other partners controlled the finance and resources, they could block any initiative they did not feel would be of benefit to the community.

It is interesting to note that many partnerships actually proceed by consensus in a more implicit way – almost by accident rather than design. Several interviewees (from all three sectors) said that the partnership board they were involved in would not vote on any issue. To do so was considered to be outside the values espoused by the partnership. Whilst no formal decision had been taken to proceed in this way, for these interviewees, partnership management implies a consensual and collegiate approach to decision-making. As one person put it:

Constitutionally, it is possible for us to proceed by majority, but we've never got to that point. The general view is that if we have to vote on an issue, we have failed. I think if you got to the point where a conflict was so bad you needed to vote, you'd have lost your legitimacy.

Advice on dealing with conflicts and disputes under such a system of governance is presented in the section on conflict resolution, page 49.

page 49.

KEY LESSONS

Attention needs to be paid to the composition of the board and the means by which all members are enabled to feel equal partners. Decision-making by consensus tends to be favoured in partnerships and helps to increase perceptions of equality of status internally and fair representation externally.

Performance of the board

Before leaving this discussion about the role of the partnership board, it is worth noting two further issues that were raised by many interviewees. These concern:

- the ability of board members to fulfil their obligations

- reviewing the performance of the board.

In some cases, the constitution and legal form of the partnership prescribes what is required and expected of board members. In others, the 'role description' emerges over time. Whichever, in order to ensure that individuals are able to fulfil these roles there may be a need for training and development of the partners in some or all of the following areas:

- 'process skills' and 'task skills' to enable the partnership to run efficiently

- knowledge about a wide range of issues from the legal duties of partnerships to information about grant regimes

- confidence and ability to communicate on equal terms with other members of the partnership.

It is frequently assumed that only people from the community and voluntary sectors will need support in developing their skills and confidence to operate in a partnership. This assumption ignores the fact that partnership management requires a specific set of competencies that include an ability to operate in environments that do not respect traditional relationships and hierarchies. Several interviewees suggested that all partnership board members need to undergo a 'cultural transformation' in order to think and operate within new structures, frameworks and processes. If this transformation is to take place, the partnership board should think carefully about how best to induct, train and develop members from all three sectors. Several providers have recognised the particular needs of partnerships and offer both public and tailored courses.[2]

A related issue that was raised by some interviewees concerned the processes by which the performance of the board might be judged. It was noted that the performance of the management team is closely measured and monitored. In many partnerships, the leader of the management team can be 'hired and fired' according to his/her success in relation to strict performance criteria. In contrast, there are generally very few mechanisms by which a partnership board might judge its own performance.

One difficulty in this respect was the voluntary nature of the role of partnership board members. Whilst this would tend to militate against formal procedures for performance appraisal, many interviewees felt it important to consider this issue.

The role of the management team

The management team is the term this report uses to describe the staff who carry out the day-to-day management of the partnership's activities. For some initiatives, this might be only one person who will co-ordinate the work of a number of other agencies acting for the partnership. In other instances, the management team might comprise a large number of people – one partnership included in this study had 12 full-time employees in its management team.

The role of the management team has been variously described by interviewees as that of facilitator, co-ordinator, initiator and implementor. In broad terms, its purpose is to implement the agenda that is set by the partnership board by translating the policies of the partnership into specific actions. This is likely to involve functions such as planning, contracting and resource management. The management team will also usually be responsible for monitoring, assessing and reporting the progress of all the partnership's activities to the board.

In a less formal capacity, interviewees suggested that the management team should also be able to act as the honest broker or the intermediary between the partners on the board. The leader of the management team should take time to understand each partner's powers and functions and the constraints under which they operate, and bring the partners together in a way that helps get the best result.

'Ownership' of the management team

Not surprisingly, many interviewees stressed the importance of the management team remaining impartial and independent. An important question in this respect is the funding of the management team. The leader of the management team will generally be a paid employee; so too might some or all of its staff.

This has the potential to upset the balance of power within the partnership if one dominant partner is the employer of the management team or funds the activities of the management team. In such circumstances, this partner's voice can be perceived as carrying the greatest weight in prescribing the activities of the partnership.

One potential solution to this problem is for the partnership to constitute itself as a limited company; then the partnership board (as joint directors in the initiative) are joint employers of the management team.

Where the members of the management team are not employees of the partnership, there is still room for potential conflicts and tensions. For example, several interviewees suggested that if the management team is made up of secondees, there is a danger that they might act to the agenda of their 'home organisation'. The question was raised, how will a secondee perform in a situation where there is a conflict of interest between what is best for the partnership and what is best for his/her employer?

Other interviewees highlighted the importance of considering where the management team is physically located.

Again, if the management team is 'attached to' one particular partner, it is less likely to be seen to be impartial and independent.

In essence, the fear expressed by interviewees was that as long as the management team of a partnership is (for whatever reason) seen to be close to one partner, then that partner will be the most powerful influence in transcribing policy decisions into action. The experience of the case study partnerships does, however, suggest that these are problems of perception rather than fact, and management team leaders we interviewed all stressed that they were aware of the issue and go to great lengths to ensure that their actions appear 'neutral'.

KEY LESSONS

In deciding upon the constitution, framework and organisational structure of the initiative, all partners must be aware of the potential implications of such decisions as where is the management team located, who funds it, and to whom does it report?

Relations between the management team and the board

In considering the organisational structure of a partnership, one issue of concern is the relationship between the management team and the board. Because it is charged with implementing policy decisions, the management team is potentially in a position to take actions 'on the ground' without any reference to the partnership board. It is possible that the power base could shift from the board to the management team.

In theory, whilst the management team has resources in terms of people and access to funds, it cannot speak for or make commitments on behalf of the partners – whether the community, the local authority or local businesses. Ultimately, the partnership board retains the decision-making power.

A small number of interviewees pointed out that in practice, however, the management team is able to develop proposals in a manner that makes it easier for the various partners to consider them – to present them and communicate them in such a way that the partnership board is more likely to approve them. There was some ambivalence amongst interviewees on this point. On the one hand, meetings go more smoothly and business seems to be dealt with more efficiently. On the other hand, it can give rise to a situation where being an employee of an organisation can be more powerful than being a board member. In virtually every partnership studied, it is the leader of the management team who has the power to set the agenda of the board meetings. In so doing, he/she has the potential to influence the scope and direction of the partnership.

An important element in this respect (and one that is rarely spoken about) is the motivations of the management team and the individual ambitions of those that work within it. Perhaps the closest this study got to this issue is reflected in the comment of one partnership manager who said:

> It is clear that the partnership has a finite life linked to the availability of funding. From my point of view, I don't want to leave a smaller organisation, I want to build the partnership so that I am able to move on.

Clearly this is a double-edged sword. On one level, the management team can be seen as working for the greater good of the partnership. At another level, it can be thought that the management team might have its own agenda above and beyond that of the partnership board.

In raising these issues, it is important to clarify precisely what interviewees were reporting. No one was claiming that in their experience a management team had actually abused its powers in any way. However, this issue was recognised as a potential area of difficulty in partnership management.

Apart from the potential tensions that can arise in internal relations, interviewees also identified external problems of public perception. Whom do the local community see as being the true representatives of 'the partnership': those that initiate actions (the management team) or those that plan the strategy (the partnership board)? The partnership board is always likely to remain less visible in the public eye than the management team that is responsible for the day-to-day activities of the initiative.

Connected with this issue of public perception is the practical point of job titles. When the head of the management team is called the Chief Executive of the partnership (as many are), it is perhaps not surprising that outsiders see this individual as leading and controlling the initiative. One partnership included in this study recognised this and chose instead the title of Secretary, reinforcing the fact that the role of the management team is to facilitate the activities of the partnership, not direct them.

The message from many of the partnerships we studied was to be clear about what is being delegated from the board to the management team. Regular contact between at least the chair and the head of the management team was seen as vital to ensuring that boundaries were understood and that there was clarity as to what was expected of the management team. This quality and quantity of contact is not always easy to achieve, especially where board members have many other claims on their time, but it seems to pay off in the long run in terms of fewer misunderstandings and misgivings.

KEY LESSONS

The relationship between the board and the management team is the key to ensuring that intentions with regard to representation and accountability are turned into reality. Clarity about the extent to which powers are delegated to the management team is vital. Attention to job titles within management teams can be useful in managing external perceptions as to who leads the partnership.

The role of committees, subcommittees and steering groups

The role of the various committees and steering groups that a partnership might choose to establish is the most difficult to define – largely because such groups can carry out a number of different functions. At one level, they exist solely to inform the board of the views and opinions of some of the key stakeholders in the work of the partnership.

At the other extreme, they are charged with identifying issues, setting agendas and influencing the strategic direction of the partnership. In order to carry out this role,

elected representatives from these committees will, by right, be members of the partnership board.

Usually, committees are set up around particular geographical, topic-based or interest-based groups. Their role is to consider in greater detail particular aspects of the broader agenda of the partnership.

It is at this level that the partnership can 'get right' issues of access, representation and equality. This arm of the partnership is often the mechanism by which a wide range of individuals and organisations can participate in defining problems, identifying responses and setting the agenda of the initiative. In practice, this generally means it is this conduit through which the views, opinions and aspirations of the community and voluntary sector pass.

The operation of committees

As the preceding discussions in Chapters 1 and 2 implied, the precise nature of the structures by which the community is represented within the partnership at this level will depend upon the partnership's aims with regard to *purpose* and *participation*. Is it the aim of the partnership to inform the community, to consult with them, or to involve them in the governance of the initiative? Assuming that the aim is to achieve the latter objective, there are two issues that need to be considered in the management and functioning of these committees.

The first is, quite simply, that the members of the committees must have equal access to all the information available to other partnership board members in order to make informed decisions. Whilst on the face of it this is a fairly straight-forward statement, experience suggests that in practice information is a lever of power that many partners are unwilling to relinquish.

Secondly, members of the committees must have the capacity to operate effectively in this role. Those people who are interested in becoming involved in committees, liaison groups or task forces may feel unable to do so because of lack of confidence. One interview described what seems to be a common problem:

> The people who put themselves forward tend to be those who are confident and articulate – you have to be to come along and speak at a meeting full of people who are often highly paid professionals. There is no doubt that local people have skills, but the issue is to make sure they are properly supported. I have seen people sent as representatives and it is unfair, they're put in a situation they have no experience of, and it just destroys what confidence they do have.

Most interviewees agreed that the prior level of community development had a significant impact on the extent to which widespread community representation could be achieved. Some initiatives had paid attention in the early stages of work to capacity building within the community, providing training in such skills as running meetings, dealing with officials and understanding planning procedures. In some instances, paid community workers were appointed to work alongside local people. The effectiveness of this tactic seems, however, to be dependent on a number of factors, including the skill of the worker and the community's previous experience of participative interventions. We heard some real success stories – including one of a group of under-16s successfully bidding for National Lottery funding for a 'cyber-café' – but also examples of

apathy increasing because the community worker was seen to be responsible for putting forward the local viewpoint.

In addition to the skills needed to operate effectively in partnerships, several interviewees highlighted other factors that present potential 'barriers to involvement' in an initiative at this level.

The first of these concern the location and timing of meetings. Committee meetings, especially those that are open to the public, should be held on different days of the week and at different times of the day to allow people to juggle their personal commitments. Thought should also go into where such meetings are held, what expenses might be incurred by attending, and what needs people might have in terms of childcare or transport.

In some cases, these practical difficulties are compounded by external pressures. A partnership member from a local authority criticised the SRB bidding schedule for restricting access to participation by local people:

> We work hard to involve a very broad spectrum of people – and we have succeeded in generating a lot of interest. But the fact that the bid has to be worked up over the school summer holiday period makes it very difficult for people with childcare responsibilities to have an input into that. It's just one of the ways that the rhetoric of partnership in SRB doesn't match the day-to-day realities.

In addition, the style of meetings was also considered to be important. Many interviewees suggested that formal meetings might not be the best fora for encouraging dialogue and involvement. It is perhaps more appropriate for this arm of the partnership to establish less formal networks of communication.

Language is again important, as one interviewee pointed out:

> You tend to lapse into jargon, using initials for things. Because you talk about things that you are involved with everyday, it is easy to assume everyone knows what you are talking about. We do need to think about the terminology we use at meetings and make it accessible for everyone.

When dealing with communities for whom English is not their first language, such problems are compounded.

Another issue is the opportunity costs involved in attending committee meetings. For many in the public and private sectors, their role in a partnership is explicitly recognised by their employers and they have a specific brief to carry out this work. For people from the community and the voluntary sector, such work is often an additional commitment that has to be fitted around a full-time job.

Because of this, partnerships need to avoid creating a small élite of community representatives. All too often, the demands of participating at this level in the partnership mean that this role falls to a small number of people who attend all the committee meetings and try to involve themselves in all the work of the partnership. This has the potential to create what one interviewee called the 'community superheroes'.

Finally, it is important to recognise that representatives of the three sectors will work to different time-scales. The very system by which committees operate – involving more people in a wider consultative process – will slow down the decision-making process. Whilst frustrating for those who are used to being able to take decisions on the spot, this must be recognised by all members of the partnership board as an inherent part of working with local communities.

KEY LESSONS

If committee structures are the means by which a partnership seeks to involve a broader section of the community in its activities, there may be a need for initial investment in skills development. There will also be a continuing need to pay attention to issues of access – both physical and information-based.

Other organisational structures

The preceding description of the organisational structure of a partnership is not meant to suggest that this is the only approach to issues of governance and management, rather that attention to structure and constitution is vital for effective partnership working.

That said, interviewees were keen to stress that it is possible to be overly concerned about the structure in which a partnership is managed and to lose sight of the real purpose of the initiative. As one person from a local authority put it:

> A partnership can benefit from flexibility in its structure. We need to concentrate on outputs rather than processes.

This view was endorsed by another interviewee who said:

> In some partnerships I have worked with, it becomes more important to handle the process properly and make sure that everyone conforms

and has a place, than it does to actually get on with the job. There have been times the partnership has fallen foul of that, and things get dropped or fragmented or diluted in the process of conforming to the demands of the structure. People lose sight of their objectives.

At the heart of this issue seems to be the fear that time spent on preparing for and attending meetings of the partnership is time diverted from running projects and getting things done. Whilst there is obviously an element of truth in this, the greater danger is that without formal structures and procedures there is more scope for confrontation and dispute. It is to these issues that we now turn.

Conflict resolution

Whilst the very word 'partnership' conjures up images of harmony and unity, the practice of working in partnership is often very different, as illustrated by the following quote from a board member:

A partnership isn't about warm feelings towards one another. A partnership is a way of getting something done, and in order to get things done you occasionally have to have a bit of confrontation or a difference of opinion. A partnership resolves those issues, and accepts that there is going to be conflict, accepts that there is going to be disagreement, but pushes ahead nonetheless. It doesn't let the whole process go down. I think partnerships are there to get results, not a place to go to have meetings and everyone has a nice cup of tea and a chat. Partnerships can be very confrontational.

Individual partners do not need to be in complete agreement on every issue. Indeed, given that by their very nature they bring together people from different sectors, it would be surprising if conflicts did not arise. The experience of the partnerships studied suggests that whilst resolution of conflict is always desirable, it is not always possible.

The trick is to focus on the 90 per cent on which you can all agree, not waste time on the 10 per cent where you're never going to see eye to eye.

In getting to the '90 per cent', a great deal of work may be needed. Perhaps the most important lesson that this research can pass on is that related by one interviewee who said:

Interpersonal skills are the secret weapon of a successful partnership management process.

Nowhere are these skills more needed than in resolving internal disputes and conflicts within the partnership board. Time and again, interviewees stressed that it is the ability of individuals to make effective interventions in the management of the partnership that enables the initiative to progress, despite differences of opinion. It was widely agreed that technical knowledge about the domain of the partnership is secondary to the personal skills of diplomacy, mediation and negotiation. Our interviewees were almost unanimous in saying that what makes the partnership management process work is the interaction of individuals; several were able to offer some concrete advice on how to overcome conflicts in the partnership process.

Firstly, it is important to recognise why disputes arise within partnerships. Often, history and politics combine to entrench the different groups around the table in traditional camps, each seeing the other as 'the enemy'. For example, community representatives are often accused of adopting an anti-business position. In such instances, it is important to look beyond the organisation represented and seek to communicate with the individual. As one interviewee put it:

> I learned to use the word compromise and try to get along; to know the individual as opposed to the organisation. Because each organisation has an image, background and position. But each individual has their own style and approach.

Secondly, all interviewees stressed that it is imperative that people look at the differences between the partners and work to overcome them. Trying to pretend that different values and outlooks do not exist was universally felt to be both naïve and unhelpful. When values are different, the only way to accommodate change is to get people to talk around their perceptions and why they hold them – are they based on direct experience, prejudice or hearsay? Only by directly addressing such issues can the partnership progress. This process was described by one person in the following way:

> I think from that one meeting there was a turning point in the partnership. The meeting generated a lot of anger and animosity, and the frankness which all sides expressed their views was quite refreshing. Nobody was prepared any longer to sit back and hide behind their organisation. It was very, very encouraging.

A third important element in conflict resolution is the ability to compromise. For example, if one of the partners backs a proposal which it originally rejected, the other partners must accommodate this change. One must allow people to save face when reaching a compromise.

Finally, partnership management is about 'playing to each other's strengths'. Representatives from each of the sectors must recognise the skills and abilities of others. The partnership is unlikely to succeed if people are trying to out do each other by demonstrating that one group alone can 'deliver the goods'.

KEY LESSONS

One cannot ignore the importance of interpersonal skills in any management process. These are skills which can be taught and can be acquired. If people who are involved in the partnership do not possess them, there is a need for training and development.

But skills cannot be bolted on where there is no willingness to be open about one's own position or to the different views of others. Here, the lessons relating to selection of partners in Chapter 2 (page 25) are vital.

Informal decision-making structures

Finally in this chapter, we turn to an issue that lurks in the shadows of any discussion about organisational structures and management processes – the fact that decisions are sometimes taken without any reference to the formal framework of the partnership.

In considering the nature of informal decision-making processes, it is important to recognise that this practice was not universally condemned by interviewees. There is a strong, pragmatic view that informal relations between partners are the 'lubricant' that oils the wheels of the formal structures and procedures of the partnership. One quote illustrates this point:

> I think the success depends on the way of working and the personalities of the individuals. One of the partners can phone me up and ask 'What do you think of this? Is it something the partnership might be interested in? How can we progress it?' Or they might phone me in advance of a board meeting if there is an issue to be resolved. So there is that degree of trust and confidence which makes me more willing to take ideas or to give the right sort of reactions back. It avoids the feeling of being ambushed. I can arrange a meeting between myself and community people in advance of a board meeting, so when these issues come up, instead of them rounding on me we can resolve it in advance, just quietly understand each other's position. And it works. By and large, it's much more effective.

This quote suggests that good, informal working relations between partners will lead to a more effective decision-making process. At one level, this is little more than an extension of the notion that partnership management requires good communication and negotiating skills. This scenario reinforces the view that partners should be open and honest with each other and work at resolving differences both within the formal structures of the partnership and outside them.

However, there is a risk that these informal relations will become secretive, exclusive, and run counter to the whole notion of partnership. At this level, access to decision-making will be influenced by factors such as personality, experience, familiarity with 'political' procedures, expertise, access to resources, etc.

The formal structures and procedures can be circumvented and power will lie in the hands of a small cabal of well-informed and well-connected individuals. In this scenario, the work of the partnership gets 'fixed' outside the board meetings when partners get down to talking one-to-one or in small groups. Those who are perceived to be less powerful or less influential will be excluded from this process. It is worth noting that suspicions of 'fixing' are not confined within any one sector; amongst our interviewees, representatives of all three sectors expressed the view that people from other sectors engaged in more informal 'politicking' than they themselves did.

KEY LESSONS

Partners must be aware that any formal organisational structure will inevitably have an informal shadow. A partnership is no different. The skill is to use informal networks, links and alliances to build positive relations between all the different partners. If these informal relations are open and accessible to all, then the process will reinforce the values and ethos of the partnership.

Notes

1   For example the National Council for Voluntary Organisations, the Voluntary and Community Division of the Department for National Heritage, the Charity Commission and local CVS offices.
2   These include the Community Development Foundation and the Civic Trust Regeneration Unit.

5 Implementing action, measuring success and planning for the future

Introduction

Once a partnership has developed its vision and mission, negotiated a plan of action and set up appropriate structures, it will be ready to implement its policies. At this stage, there will be two strands to the work of the initiative:

- the day-to-day functioning of the partnership

- the realisation of a 'bigger vision' – producing a major impact by increasing the capacity of those the partnership is working with to 'help themselves'.

In many respects, carrying out the day-to-day operations of the partnership is usually relatively straightforward. What is more difficult is maintaining and developing what has been achieved – ensuring that new assets or resources are not simply 'bolted on' to the communities in which the partnership is working, but take root in a way that enables initial investments to be leveraged and multiply to achieve much wider benefits. Many of our interviewees suggested that this can only be done by changing the hearts and minds, and developing the skills, of people working with the partnership in the community.

Implementing action – process or task?

Throughout this report, we have avoided making judgements as to which of the partnerships we studied were most or least successful. This is partly because such judgements would necessarily be subjective. In addition, in considering the findings of this report, it is important to recognise that interviewees themselves were not in agreement over what defines a successful partnership.

When it comes to moving beyond the development stage to implementing action, there was some dispute about how partnership initiatives should operate. For some, the sole criterion of a successful partnership operation is one that meets its stated objectives and delivers beneficial outcomes to its 'target audience'.

For others, however, this measure must be tempered by a consideration of the processes by which the aims of the partnership are met. It is not enough to carry out the task and deliver outputs; the initiative must proceed in a way which is entirely compatible with the ethos of partnership.

Put simply, interviewees drew a distinction between the 'ends' and the 'means'; between outputs and processes.

This distinction can best be illustrated by example. One of the partnerships included in this report, which has been in existence for some 18 months, has concentrated its efforts on establishing local needs and prioritising areas for action. It has deliberately adopted a very open and consultative approach which has involved gathering the views and opinions of a wide cross-section of people. As yet, however, it has achieved little in terms of delivering tangible projects or programmes to address the needs it has identified.

In contrast, another initiative which has been in existence for a similar time has done much to improve the local economy. Amongst a wide range of projects, it has created an advice centre on benefits, education and training grants, and enabled several new businesses to set up by providing shop and office premises for community-based organisations. Whilst this partnership has been very strong on achieving deliverable outcomes, it might be judged to have adopted a less inclusive or consultative approach to its governance and management.

Clearly, much of the reason why these partnerships have produced different outcomes is because they have set themselves different goals. However, it is also connected to their different approaches and philosophies towards partnership management.

The first initiative explicitly recognises that the process by which results are achieved is as important as the results themselves. One interviewee stressed the need for widespread consultation and communication:

> No one partner is going to be able to address the needs of this area. We have to be absolutely clear of what the 50 or so different groups that are already there are doing, and make connections between them, before we attempt to do something that existing organisations are set up to do.

The second partnership adopts a much more direct approach that suggests, in the words of one interviewee:

> Consensus is not always a good thing – it stifles action. You need to take a risk and get things done. That can't be achieved within a bureaucratic structure.

KEY LESSONS

At one level, it is quite clear that a partnership that does not deliver a significant proportion of what it set out to achieve cannot be said to be successful.

At the other extreme, an initiative that produces real change but does so without the support and involvement of all three sectors cannot be truly described as a partnership – it is simply an entrepreneurial operation. In implementing their policies, partners must try to balance these two perspectives.

Measuring success

Regardless of which side they took in the debate as to whether the success of a partnership should be measured in terms of outputs or processes, the majority of interviewees agreed on the need for a partnership to develop transparent measures of success (both quantitative and qualitative) that judge the activities of the initiative against its stated aims and objectives.

Time and again, it was suggested that externally verifiable performance indicators will improve both internal management processes (assuming the information is used as part of a wider process of performance review) and external credibility and accountability.

Several interviewees made the point that, when attempting to measure the performance of a partnership, it is important to distinguish between three related elements:

- inputs – the resources used in terms of money, people, buildings, equipment, etc.

- outputs – the tangible products or services provided by the partnership; these might include such measures as training places provided, the number of people housed, and advice leaflets distributed

- outcomes – the more abstract achievements of the partnership; for example, a partnership working in the field of economic regeneration might seek to develop some measure of how it has improved the employment prospects of individuals living in an area.

It was generally accepted that it becomes progressively more difficult to assess each of these elements as one moves from simple input measures to the broader impact of the work of the partnership. Many interviewees complained that the majority of externally imposed performance mechanisms tend to emphasise measures of short-term inputs and outputs rather than long-term outcomes. This was felt to be especially true for those partnerships that have performance indicators set by funders. In order to comply with the requirement of many funding regimes, management time and resources are driven towards collecting and collating information about the day-to-day efficiency of the partnership's operations. As a result, there is less time to devote towards devising and implementing performance indicators that monitor the strategic growth and long-term effectiveness of the initiative.

In any event, measures that might be appropriate given a partnership's aim for long-term outcomes, may be too controversial to state publicly. Two contrasting quotes from members of partnership boards illustrate this issue:

> One of the greatest moments for me was when there was an absolute outcry from local residents over plans to replace housing stock. It was no longer just sit back and take it.

> The local people are less aggressive now towards

the local authority. There's less bolshiness now because they understand the processes that have to be gone through to deliver.

Whilst the issues raised in measuring outcomes are the more interesting, it would be wrong to play down the importance of ensuring that there are rigorous processes of internal auditing and financial accounting in place. Amongst the partnerships studied, there were several examples where such mechanisms were used as 'early warning systems' to alert the partnership executive to potential areas of difficulty. As such, they were seen as vital in avoiding failure.

However, the potential tension between short- and long-term measures of success serves to underline the fact that the circumstances of each partnership will dictate what can and cannot be measured. It is the role of the executive board and management team to decide how best to record, collate and publish data on the work of the partnership.

Before leaving this issue, it is worth noting that some interviewees advocated treating performance measurement as one small part of a wider span of quality improvement processes. These might include defining standards for the partnership management process; ensuring policies and procedures deliver to those standards; and creating systems for external recognition and verification of the principles of partnership management. This is clearly an area that requires further research, but was seen by some as representing a major step forward to improving the quality of management in cross-sectoral partnerships.

Finally, it should also be recognised that any process of performance measurement should look outwards as well as inwards. It is vitally important that the partnership should benchmark its activities against other similar initiatives.

KEY LESSONS

Measures of the inputs and outputs of an initiative, whilst time-consuming to collate, are important for the short-term management of the activities of the partnership. However, such processes must be complemented by long-term measures of achievement.

Partners should be active 'networkers' and always maintain an external focus. The executive and management team of a partnership should seek to build links across and between other initiatives in order to learn from others' experience and improve the general understanding of the issues each seeks to address.

Developing good publicity

Working well is clearly an admirable aim, but letting people know you are working well also seems to be important. Virtually all of the interviewees felt that positive media coverage can be a very valuable tool in developing the partnership. Their advice was to use whatever means possible to spread the word about the work of the initiative, with the aim of making everyone within the community feel a little bit better about themselves. As one interviewee put it:

Nobody thinks they are doing well on their own patch. When you get external recognition, through the media, it really boosts local confidence.

It was often commented that there are a large number of partnership initiatives which are doing positive work, but which do not take advantage by failing to present their achievements to the outside world in an effective way. One of the partnerships we studied had found an effective way of maximising coverage of its activities – a senior manager from the local newspaper group sat on the board.

An alternative approach to increasing awareness about the work of the initiative is to invite people to come and see what the partnership is doing. More than one of the partnerships included in this study spoke of how the kudos and credibility of their efforts had increased following an official visit by a senior politician or member of the royal family. Such an event can be a powerful magnet for encouraging high-level support and recognition, especially from members of the business community.

In essence, the message from interviewees is clear:

Constantly remind people of your successes – it all helps to contribute to a virtuous circle that makes the continual search for funds slightly easier.

Interviewees warned that without publicity and recognition, the community as a whole (both business and voluntary sectors) will tend to ascribe the work to 'the local council, central government, or perhaps another statutory body that is working in the area'.

There is an additional element to this issue of publicity which concerns the need for the partnership to be seen to be collectively responsible for successes. Time and again, interviewees stressed that it is vitally important to acknowledge the contribution of all partners, even at the simplest level of having their names on documents that talk about the initiative. There will sometimes be the temptation for one partner to claim an undue amount of credit – individuals will seek to gain credit for what the partnership does so that they have more credibility within their own organisation and can justify what they are doing. This should be avoided at all costs.

It is important, however, to recognise that media coverage of the work of a partnership does bring with it potential problems. It was suggested that a partnership initiative that concentrates on a particular geographical area runs the danger that any publicity or marketing campaign will simply highlight the inherent social or economic difficulties of that area. As one interviewee put it:

> At first, we indulged in quite an aggressive marketing campaign, highlighting the areas of work we intended to undertake. That simply served to draw attention to the problems we faced in this area, which drew more negative publicity. Now we prefer to publicise individual projects, so each success story builds on the next to slowly change public perceptions about the area.

It is perhaps worth noting that other interviewees suggested that similar problems can occur in the bidding processes for public funds. That is, a partnership initiative might feel obliged to 'play up' the nature of problems in an area in order to demonstrate that it is sufficiently 'worthy' of financial assistance. Such a process can add to general perceptions that a particular area is 'beyond hope', so adversely affecting the prospects of the community as a whole.

It is also worth mentioning that one partnership included in this study seemed unconcerned about publicity. In this case, a large number of projects were underway or successfully completed, yet there was low public awareness of the partnership's existence. One board member commented:

> I suppose it would be nice if more people were saying 'Isn't the [X] Partnership wonderful?' But, actually, what matters is that the projects are happening – facilities are being improved, the environment is starting to look cared for, job opportunities are opening up – and local groups, local firms and local people are getting the credit. In a sense, it's not important that we brought them together and enabled it to happen – people are taking pride in what they've achieved.

KEY LESSONS

Positive publicity can make life much easier for partnerships, facilitating access to funds, other resources and wider involvement. It does not come automatically and needs to be planned for, as with any other aspect of the partnership's activities. But actions speak louder than words, and a record of achievement is, in any case, the key to good PR.

Building systemic solutions

All interviewees agreed that the aim of a partnership initiative should be to move beyond fire-fighting and temporary solutions. A cross-sectoral initiative should have the power and energy to bring about permanent change in the area in which it operates. Many of the people we spoke with felt that partnership initiatives are in a unique position to tackle social, economic and environmental issues with a holistic, multifaceted approach. The necessity to address the immediate needs of a particular group should not militate against a broader agenda of systemic change.

In many circumstances, interviewees felt that the education of young people is very important in this respect. Not only should the partnership work to ameliorate the situation in a particular area; it should also use the initiative to help youngsters understand how similar problems can be avoided in the future. According to one representative from the community:

a partnership should aim to get hold of people in primary schools to teach them what citizenship means – what being public spirited is all about.

To help achieve this longer-term, wider perspective, interviewees suggested that there should be a movement encouraging people in the community to progress from small local projects to more significant issues. One interviewee described this process as:

getting people to move their efforts from the street, to the block, to the local area.

Although this particular partnership is working to achieve environmental improvements, an analogous process can take place in partnerships working with other issues. If this process is handled well, all partners (including the wider community) will naturally grow in confidence, ability, expertise and experience to be able to tackle bigger, more substantial projects.

That said, the advice of interviewees was that a partnership should aim to develop a 'balanced portfolio' of objectives. At one level,

it is important that the initiative is seen to be doing something concrete in the short-term. For this reason, it should seek to establish a number of clearly defined, easily delivered outcomes. As we have already heard, the initial enthusiasm and momentum of a partnership will be better sustained with a few 'early wins'. As one interviewee put it, 'nothing breeds success like success'.

A pragmatic, action-oriented approach may bring other benefits: several interviewees stressed that people generally want to be involved in 'making and doing things', as well as planning and designing. In Chapter 2 we recognised that in any partnership initiative there will inevitably be a degree of apathy and disinterest. It was suggested that one strategy to help overcome this is to get as many people as possible physically involved in delivering the work of the partnership.

The prior level of community development is a key factor in this respect. Where community groups, self-help groups and local action groups already exist, the whole process of developing the work of the partnership is made easier. If, however, the partnership is operating in an area where there are few or no such networks, more work will have to be done to involve the community.

Once again, it might be necessary and appropriate to offer people training so they feel more able to participate in the activities of the partnership. One of the partnerships studied made support to community organisations its first priority when initiating projects. Amongst the measures it supported were:

- grants to employ professional help, such as solicitors

- a development support worker post, focused on advising groups about funding sources, constitution and long-term development

- organisational development checks facilitated by consultants who could then help with action planning

- IT hardware and software to support administrative tasks and facilitate networking between groups.

KEY LESSONS

However it is achieved, involving the community in whatever way possible (drawing on their resources, experience, knowledge or advice) gives people a feeling of pride and ownership in the outcomes of the partnership.

Developing the long-term view

When questioned about how to implement the policies of an initiative, one of the chief concerns of the interviewees was to shift the focus of the partnership from the 'here and now' to the 'broader picture'. A question that was posed by representatives of all three sectors was 'how do you encourage others in the partnership to take a long-term view?'

Once again, the very nature of the way in which many partnerships are funded on relatively short time-scales militates against any agency adopting a strategic view of the future. This point was illustrated by one interviewee who said:

I would love to do long-term planning – I know what I want in [this community], I want to totally

restructure it. And there are some things we've introduced that will undoubtedly have a long-term impact and are safe. But on the whole, the problem is funding – it's short-term, quick fix. You can't do long-term planning because you don't know what the education budget is going to be, you don't know what the housing budget is going to be, and on it goes. There's the lottery, that's given us a boost, but essentially the best you can do on the back of any of these funding sources is medium-term planning.

The dangers of simply pursuing an implementation strategy based on making the best use of whatever funding is available in the short-term were set out by a board member from another partnership:

At the end of 10 years we will have a nice piece of paper that will say from 1989 to 1999, or whatever, we received £X million and created X number of jobs. That will be great and the various partners will go away. And then the problems will come back, because they don't have that vision. You must try to force the partnership to say 'What is happening tomorrow?'

A separate but related issue that faces partnerships in moving from the planning to the implementation stage is, how do you keep people committed, enthused and supportive? As with so many projects and initiatives, much of the 'interesting' work gets done at the outset in designing and forming the partnership. At this early stage, it is important to recognise that a partnership is not about quick fixes, but is about trying to build a structure, an attitude and values that will last a long time. Ironically, several interviewees suggested that in circumstances where the partnership does have a limited lifetime, it is easier to keep people on board because they know they are not going to get locked into an indefinite commitment.

KEY LESSONS

It is very important to recognise that part of the successful management process (funding considerations aside) must be a readiness to question the continuing viability of the initiative. Partners must be prepared to ask 'has the partnership, in this particular form, done what it set out to do?' Inevitably, there will come a time when the answer to this question is 'yes' and all partners must have prepared for this eventuality in advance.

Developing exit strategies

Most of the partnerships we studied were still at a relatively early stage in implementation and none had got so far as developing a formal exit strategy (despite the fact that one has been in existence for more than a century). Nonetheless, there was almost universal recognition that throughout the life of a partnership, there must be processes by which the initiative can continually revisit the questions and issues that were addressed at its inception and formation. As one interviewee put it:

This is not a partnership into infinity. You have to have a clear view of what you are trying to achieve, what this particular grouping of people can do, when they believe that they will have gone a long way towards doing it, and then being prepared to say 'all right something else needs doing, someone else needs to make it happen'. I think if that sort of process is in place, if you're

regularly reviewing that, then it's actually easier to keep people on board, because they know they're not going to get locked into something.

Much of the literature about partnerships and community participation suggests that an essential requirement of any initiative is to develop the knowledge, experience and abilities of community groups so they become self-managing. This view was endorsed by many of the interviewees included in this study. One explained his view thus:

As long as people believe in the vision, then the commitment should be sustainable – it's not right to think in terms of sustaining the partnership. Partnerships come together around a vision and mission, and as that changes, so the partnership sheds people, brings in new blood, but it doesn't go on ad infinitum. You have to beware of creating a situation where a partnership is seen as the only body that can bid for any sort of funding.

Most felt that the work of a partnership should build the capacity of local people to carry on the work of the initiative after the funds have run out or the other partners have 'moved on'. Interviewees suggested that 'sustainability' is about much more than surviving until the next tranche of public funds arrives. For many, a partnership should seek to empower the community to act for itself.

The essential feature of 'capacity building' and 'empowerment' is to include the community at each and every stage of the partnership development process by adopting an inclusive approach at the outset. The partnership should avoid constructing barriers to community participation and enable community representatives to experience at first hand the various aspects of partnership management. Hence, all partners need to be given the opportunity to develop and acquire the skills to:

- analyse and define the areas and issues to be addressed by the initiative

- prioritise needs

- develop a vision and mission statement

- select partners, advisors and collaborators

- understand the system – know where grants come from and how to access funding and support

- design programmes of action and the appropriate management structures to support them

- implement, monitor and assess programmes

- review and recreate the long-term strategic direction of the initiative.

The more that legitimate representatives of the community are enabled to have full and equal access to each and every stage of the partnership development process, the more likely it is that an initiative will succeed in building the capacity of the community in which it operates to sustain and build on the partnership's achievements.

That said, it is vital to recognise that real empowerment means moving a stage further by allowing the community not only to influence decision-making processes, but to command the resources that were previously in the hands of central or local government. This calls for the creation of new structures and a redefinition of what is meant by partnership. As such, if empowerment is to take place, the whole process described in this report needs to begin again with new partners and new ground rules.

It is likely that the structures appropriate for the continuation of the work of a partnership initiative, and the people involved in the creation of those structures, will face many of the same challenges experienced by those who have participated in this research study. In this way, it is hoped that many of the lessons shared by interviewees will be applicable to new audiences, who will seek to establish different initiatives and strive to achieve ever more demanding goals.

KEY LESSONS

The 'golden thread' of involvement, consultation and participation remains central if ambitions to create change that outlives the partnership are to be realised.

The lessons learned by the partnership on its journey through the development cycle seem likely to be equally applicable to those in community and other groups who seek to build on the partnership's work.

Appendix 1

Interviewees participating in the research study

Groundwork, Dearne Valley

Jack McBane, Chief Executive, Groundwork Dearne Valley

Roger Mitchell, Group Leader, Planning Department, Rotherham Borough Council

Don Chamberlain, Community Relations Managers, British Telecom plc

Colin Ward, local resident and member of Kilnhurst Local Action Group

TRAX Motor Project, Oxford

Myles Daly, Project Manager, TRAX

Steve Curran, Youth Worker, Blackbird Leys Youth Centre

Patsy Townsend, Senior Probation Officer, Oxford Probation Service

Martin Ince, Director Service Operations, Rover Cars

Peter Bridges, ex-Chair of TRAX Management Committee

Sheffield City Liaison Group

John Lambert, Secretary, Sheffield City Liaison Group

Hugh Sykes, Chairman, Sheffield Development Corporation

Pamela Gordon, Chief Executive, Sheffield City Council

David Stone, Managing Director, British Steel

Keith Davie, Chief Executive, Sheffield TEC

The Daycare Trust, London

Carol Sherriff, Director, Daycare Trust

Madeline Watson, Executive Committee member of Daycare Trust

Wester Hailes Partnership, Edinburgh

Willie Docherty, Chief Executive, Wester Hailes Partnership

Betty Glasgow, local resident and Vice-chair of Wester Hailes Representative Council

Andy Milne, Co-ordinator, Wester Hailes Representative Council

Graham Crawford, Chair, Business Support Group

Ed Weeple, Under Secretary of State, The Scottish Office

Cllr Willie Dunn, Edinburgh District Council

David Crichton, Director of Projects, LEEL

Broxtowe Small Area Regeneration Partnership, Nottingham

Neil Horsley, Nottingham Development Enterprise

Gill Harrison, Nottingham Development Enterprise

Cllr Graham Chapman, Nottingham City Council

Phil Whittaker, local resident

Maggie Grimshaw, Policy Officer, Nottingham City Council

Moss Side and Hulme Community Development Trust, Manchester

Tom Nelson, Chairman of the Board, Moss Side and Hulme Community Development Trust

Chris Woodcock, Kellogg Company of Great Britain and member of the Business Support Group

Manchester University Settlement

Hillary Brooke, Director, Manchester University
     Settlement
Professor Brian Robson, Chair, Manchester
     University Settlement
Veronica Powell, local resident
Alison Milner, Chief Executive's Office,
     Manchester City Council
Bob Young, Co-operative Bank

The Netherton Partnership, Liverpool

Jim Flynn, Chair, The Netherton Partnership
Mike Swift, Chief Executive, Sefton Chamber of
     Commerce and Industry
Simon Ryder, Strategy and Policy Manager, TEC
David Brennan, Partnership Manager, The
     Netherton Partnership

Ebor Gardens Partnership, Leeds

Simon Littlejohn, Group Community Affairs
     Manager, Yorkshire Water plc
Sally Wright, Assistant Director, Leeds City
     Council
John Cronin, Community Affairs Manager,
     Yorkshire Post Newspapers
Judith Robinson, Manager, Leeds Education 2000
Denise Ragan, Executive Liason Officer, Ebor
     Gardens Partnership

Shirebrook District Development Trust, Derbyshire

Stephen Fritchley, Chief Finance Officer
Ian Lodder, Rural Development Commission
Lindsay Townsend, North Derbyshire TEC

Mansfield Diamond Partnership

Wynne Garnet, Mansfield CVS
Jim Hawkins, Leader, Mansfield District
     Council
Carmel Heathcote, Mansfield Diamond
     Partnership
Abbey Johnson, North Nottingham TEC
Stan Crawford, Mansfield and Woodhouse
     Community Development Group
Chris Collison, Director of Planning and
     Economic Development, Mansfield District
     Council

'External advisors'

Caroline Clark, Programme Director, Civic Trust
     Regeneration Unit
Dr Richard Simmons, Chief Executive, Dalston
     City Partnership Ltd
June Lightfoot, Regional Manager South East,
     Community Development Foundation
David Wilcox, Managing Director, Partnership
     Limited

(Note: the research study has taken 18 months to complete. During the life of the project, some interviewees have changed posts. The above list gives details at the time that interviews took place.)

Appendix 2

Partnerships studied

The purpose of this appendix is to provide a more detailed overview of the range of different partnership initiatives included in this study. Each short profile (presented in alphabetical order) is intended to give a flavour of the scope, objectives and purpose of each partnership.

Broxtowe Small Area Regeneration Partnership, Nottingham

The Broxtowe estate is a 1930s housing development of some 2,000 homes (6,000 people) on the north-eastern edge of Nottingham city centre. The Broxtowe Small Area Regeneration Partnership came out of a general recognition by city leaders of the need to adopt a multiagency approach to some of the problems of crime, poor housing and lack of employment opportunities on the estate.

The partnership comprises 20 different partners representing all three sectors. Its work is overseen by five subgroups responsible for initiatives in the following areas: employment, training and community enterprise; children and young people; health, community and under-eights; housing and environment; and education. One arm of the partnership, the Broxtowe Steering Group, recently submitted an unsuccessful bid for funds under the Single Regeneration Budget.

The Daycare Trust, London

The Daycare Trust was formed as a charitable organisation in 1989 by the National Childcare Campaign which lobbied for extended provision of public sector nursery care. Originally, the major service it provided was information on childcare provision in both public and private sectors.

By the 1990s, technological advances coupled with progress made by similar organisations in the USA led the Daycare Trust to investigate a partnership model with local authority and private sector support. Childcare Links was a particular initiative that was set up to forge such cross-sectoral partnerships. In essence, a Childcare Link provides information and advice, helps to develop childcare facilities, and promotes quality standards in childcare provision in specific local areas.

There are now about 30 Childcare Link initiatives throughout the UK, about half of which the Daycare Trust has been instrumental in establishing. Once established, they are independent bodies drawing funding from across the sectors.

Ebor Gardens Partnership, Leeds

This partnership was established in 1994 as a business-led initiative that aims to work with the residents of the Ebor Gardens estate in Leeds on a range of social, economic and environmental projects. Impetus was given to the partnership development process following a visit to the area by HRH the Prince of Wales in June 1995.

To date, the partnership has concentrated its efforts on establishing local needs and prioritising areas for action. It is currently seeking funds to make physical improvements to the local community centre and children's playground. The partnership – which comprises representatives from the business sector, Leeds City Council, Leeds Education 2000 and the community – is an unincorporated association. It is trying to obtain charitable status in an effort to gain improved access to funding opportunities.

Groundwork, Dearne Valley

This initiative was linked to the City Challenge bid put forward in 1991 by the Dearne Valley Partnership. David Trippier, the government minister responsible at the time, stipulated that City Challenge funding would only be forthcoming if a Groundwork Trust was established in the area. Although the three local authorities (Barnsley, Doncaster and Rotherham) initially agreed, this has since caused some tension.

Groundwork Dearne Valley is an independent charity that is run and controlled by its board. This board is made up of eight members: three representatives from the local authorities; representatives from BT, Allied Domecq and the Co-operative Bank; a local resident; and a representative of the Dearne Valley Partnership. It is working to improve the environmental, social and economic environment in an area of South Yorkshire that has suffered greatly from the decline of traditional coal and steel industries.

Manchester University Settlement

In 1995, the Manchester University Settlement (MUS) celebrated its centenary year. Throughout its history, one of its aims has been to encourage staff and students of the university to work with members of the local community.

Working in partnership with representatives from the public, private and voluntary sectors, the agenda of the MUS currently covers a range of issues centred around the major themes of

community development, young people and housing. Specific initiatives include an outdoor pursuits project, care and repair (a home improvement agency which provides practical help for owner-occupiers and private tenants), the young people's housing project (a self-build housing scheme), and the Beswick and Bradford Community Project.

Mansfield Diamond Partnership

The Mansfield Diamond Partnership developed in response to the announcement of the pit closure programme, which drew together several statutory and voluntary agencies around a common cause. Shortly afterwards, the government announced the creation of the Single Regeneration Budget. The partnership successfully bid for the first round of SRB funds and (inclusive of matching resources) the bid totals some £50 million delivered through 86 projects.

This initial bid was prepared by a core team of representatives from the Mansfield Community Volunteer Service, Mansfield District Council, North Nottinghamshire Training and Enterprise Council and Nottinghamshire County Council. This core team is represented on the board of the partnership together with a community representative and two private sector representatives.

The concept of the 'diamond partnership' comes from the different facets of the initiative which includes work in business development, education and training; environmental issues; crime and safety; infrastructure; and a package of measures aimed at Mansfield Woodhouse, a disadvantaged community in the area.

Moss Side and Hulme Community Development Trust, Manchester

The Moss Side and Hulme area of Manchester is home to nearly 40,000 people from a broad range of racial, ethnic and social backgrounds. The area has been the subject of a number of renewal programmes over the past 20 years. Over time, the area has become associated (wrongly, many would say) with images of crime, drugs, poverty and unemployment.

In the late 1980s, despairing of having yet another initiative 'done to them', a group of local people and business representatives came together with a proposal for a community-led economic regeneration agency. With the financial support of the government's task force, this later became the Moss Side and Hulme Community Development Trust (CDT).

The CDT is an independent, non-profit-making, cross-sectoral partnership that has three strategic aims: local wealth creation; community empowerment; and financial independence and self-sufficiency. These three aims are translated into a series of nine key objectives.

The Netherton Partnership, Liverpool

The Netherton area of Liverpool has a population of around 24,000. The Netherton Partnership was established in 1994 and has successfully bid for SRB funds. It is an unincorporated association whose partnership board comprises 14 members: the Netherton Community Forum (5); the Netherton Business Group (4); Sefton Council (3); Merseyside TEC (1); and Sefton Health (1).

The vision and strategic objectives of the partnership are achieved through a series of programmes and individual projects, each of which report to and are advised by one of five steering groups. The five areas of activities comprise education, training and employment; housing; community safety, crime prevention and youth provision; the environment, recreation and leisure; and care, health and community support.

The Sheffield City Liaison Group, Sheffield

In the late 1970s, Sheffield saw a rapid rise in unemployment brought about by the decline of the traditional industries in the city. The Sheffield Economic Regeneration Group was set up in response to these pressures and this, in turn, developed the Sheffield Partnership 2000 and the Sheffield Development Corporation.

In the autumn of 1992, the appointment of new leaders to the City Council and the Sheffield Development Corporation led to the setting up of the Sheffield City Liaison Group. Essentially, this is an enabling and facilitating group; it does not carry out tasks but sets the strategic agenda for the economic and social regeneration of the city. The group comprises senior representatives of Chambers of Commerce and Industry, the City Council, Sheffield Development Corporation, Sheffield Hallam University, Sheffield Health Authority, Sheffield TEC, the University of Sheffield and the Company of Cutlers.

Shirebrook District Development Trust, Derbyshire

The Shirebrook District Development Trust was set up in 1994 in response to colliery closures in order to give advice to local people and support for local businesses. It is now the key delivery mechanism for a number of initiatives, some of which are supported by SRB funding. These include an advice centre on benefits, education and training; grant support and advice to local businesses including community enterprises; local regeneration through the acquisition of shop and office premises for community-based organisations; and the support of a town farm based at the local school. The trust also prints and distributes a monthly newsletter that is delivered to 7,500 homes in the area.

The trust is a non-profit-making company, limited by guarantee. It sees self-sufficiency as an important goal and owns a number of properties throughout the town. These generate a significant income stream, albeit from low or subsidised rents.

The TRAX Motor Project, Oxford

TRAX grew out of a probationary service initiative that was set up in the summer of 1991 in response to the rise in car crime in the Oxford area. Two months later came the highly publicised disturbances on the Blackbird Leys estate, raising public awareness about the issue.

The Chief Superintendent of the police called a meeting of senior members of local government and the social services. They approved the proposed motor project initiative and began to seek funding from the Home Office and the private sector. The management committee of

TRAX is made up of representatives from the police, social services, the probation service and local businesses including Rover, Unipart and Fox FM (the local radio station).

TRAX is a registered charity and a limited company. Its mission is 'to channel the natural enthusiasm of young people for vehicles into a positive and challenging direction, to aid their development towards further achievement'.

Wester Hailes Partnership, Edinburgh

The Wester Hailes Partnership (WHP) is one of four area-based initiatives established following the publication in 1988 of the Scottish Office document *New Life for Urban Scotland*. It was launched in the following year after a period of preparatory work by the community and the major partners.

The partnership board comprises 17 representatives made up as follows: community (5); Edinburgh District Council (2); Lothian Regional Council (2); the Scottish Office (2); LEEL, the Local Enterprise Council (1); Scottish Homes (1); private sector (2); Lothian Health Board (1); and the Employment Agency (1).

The WHP has a number of goals in seven discrete areas: housing; employment; social policy; community facilities and environment; economic development; community ownership; and image of the area. The work of the partnership is serviced by a resource team of some six people who operate on a £0.5 million budget provided by the Scottish Office.

Bibliography

Bidding Guidance: A Guide to Bidding for Resources from the Government's Single Regeneration Budget, The Challenge Fund (1995) HMSO, London

'Business Partnerships – a New Opportunity', *NEEDIS* (1990) Vol. 1, No. 3, Autumn

'Sweeping the Changes: Dearne Valley', *Corporate Location UK Urban Areas Supplement* (1993)

Good Funding Practice (1994) Recommendations from a conference of North East funders held at Lumley Castle, Country Durham in November 1994, Tyne and Wear Foundation, Newcastle-upon-Tyne

Guidelines to the Community Involvement Aspect of the SRB Challenge Fund (1995) Regeneration and the Community, Community Development Foundation, London, April

Leicester City Challenge – Developing Community Entrepreneurs (1994) The Dragon Awards, the Lord Mayor of London's Awards for Business Involvement in the Community, BITC, London

'Major Sees Exemplary Crime Prevention Project Based on Community Partnership', *Reuters Business Briefing*, 10 February 1995

Meeting the Challenge of Change: Voluntary Action into the 21st Century (1996) Report of the Commission on the Future of the Voluntary Sector, NCUO, London

New Life for Urban Scotland (1988) The Scottish Office/HMSO, Edinburgh

The Individual and the Community: The Role of the Voluntary Sector (1992) The Home Office and the Central Office of Information, London

Armstrong, John and Henderson, Paul (eds) (1992) *Putting the Community into Community Care*, Community Development Foundation, London

Bell, John (1992) *Community Development Teamwork: Measuring the Impact*, Community Development Foundation, London

Buffton, Barbara (1994) *Working Together for the Future: Education-Business Partnerships*, Industrial Relations Review and Report, No. 568

Buss, Terry and Bartok, Robert (1994) 'Corby, England Leads Economic Development in Europe', *Economic Development Review*, Vol. 12, No. 3

Campbell, Andrew and Tawadey, Kiran (1990) *Mission and Business Philosophy*, Butterworth-Heinemann, London

Campbell, Andrew and Yeung, Sally (1990) *Do You Have a Mission Statement?* Economist Publications, London

Chanan, Gabriel (1992) *Out of the Shadows: Local Community Action and the European Community*, European Foundation for the Improvement of Living and Working Conditions, Dublin

Chanan, Gabriel and Vos, Koos (1989) *Social Change and Local Action: Coping with Disadvantage in Urban Areas*, European Foundation for the Improvement of Living and Working Conditions, Dublin

Christie, Ian (1991) *Profitable Partnerships: An Action Guide for Company Investment in the Community*, Policy Studies Institute, London

Christie, Ian *et al.* (1991) *Profitable Partnerships: A Report on Business Investment in the Community*, Policy Studies Institute, London

Community Development Foundation (1994) *Community Involvement in Urban Regeneration*, a Study for the European Commission (DGXVI), August 1994

Community Enterprise Awards (1994) *Community Oracle: Revealing Good Practice in Community Enterprise and Partnership for the Social Economy*, Business in the Community, Durham University and Tioxide UK, London

Deakin, Nicholas (1991) 'Government and the Voluntary Sector in the 1990s', *Policy Studies*, Vol. 12., No. 3, Autumn

Dew, Maggie and Stone, Judith (1992) *Setting up Voluntary Sector Partnerships in Daycare: A Step-by-Step Guide*, Voluntary Organisations Liaison Council for Under Fives, London

Fazey, Ian Hamilton (1994) 'Survey of Merseyside (2): partnership tackles region's image – how companies have been persuaded to put their money where their mouths are', *Financial Times*, 14 July

Field, P. *et al.* (1995) *Local Development of Partnerships and Investments in People*, Employment Department Research Series No. 51, May

Finn, Dan (1994) *A New Partnership? Training and Enterprise Councils and the Voluntary Sector*, London Boroughs Grants Committee, London

Haughton, G., Hart, T., Strange, I., Thomas, K. and Peck, J. (1995) *TECs and their Non-employer Stakeholders*, Employment Department, Sheffield

Hazell, Robert and Whybrew, Ted (eds) (1993) *Resourcing the Voluntary Sector: The Funders' Perspective*, the Association of Charitable Foundations, London

Hutchinson, Jo and Foley, Paul (1994) 'Partnerships in Local Economic Development: The Management Issues', *Management Research News*, Vol. 17, No. 7

Huxham, Chris (1993) *Collaborative Capability and Collaborative Maturity*, Management Research News, Vol. 17, No. 7

Johnson, G. and Scholes, K. (1993) *Exploring Corporate Strategy*, Prentice-Hall, London

Knight, Barry (1992) *Voluntary Action: Executive Summary*, Centris, London

Landry, Charles and Mulgan, Geoff (1994) *Themes and Issues: The Future of the Charities and the Voluntary Sector*, Working Paper 1, Demos, London

Lawless, Paul (1991) *Public-Private Sector Partnerships in the United Kingdom*, Working Paper No. 16, Sheffield Hallam University, Sheffield

Leat, Diana (1993) *Managing across Sectors: Similarities and Differences between For-profit and Voluntary Non-profit Organisations*, City University Business School, London

Lloyd-Jones, Hugh (1994) 'Storm Clouds on the Horizon', *Training Tomorrow*, July

Martin, Steve (1994) *Economic Partnership, Community and the Local Authority (Proceedings of a Two Day Workshop, Aston University, Birmingham, 17–18 February 1994)*, The Local Government Management Board

McFarlane, Richard and Laville, Jean-Louis (1992) *Developing Community Partnerships in Europe*: *New Ways of Meeting Social Needs in Europe*, The Directory of Social Change and The Calouste Gulbenkian Foundation, London

Obeng, Eddie and Crainer, Stuart (1994) *Making Re-engineering Happen*, Pitman, London

Opie, Andrew (1991) 'Compact Storms the Inner Cities', *Employment Gazette*, November

Palmer, Caroline (1994) 'Charity at Work', *Accountancy Age*, 15 December

Patten, The Rt Hon John MP (1991) *Government, Business and the Voluntary Sector: A Developing Partnership*, Policy Studies Institute, London

Phaure, Steven (1994) *The 'P' Word: Partnerships between Local Government and the Voluntary Sector in London*, London Voluntary Service Council, London

Rollison, Richard (1993) 'Facing the Challenge', *Training Tomorrow*

Rounthwaite, Tony (1994a) 'Changing Token Joint Working into Successful Service Partnership', *Managing Service Quality*, Vol. 4, No. 2

Rounthwaite, Tony (1994b) 'Partnerships in the Public Sector', *Managing Service Quality*, Vol. 4, No. 3

Rowley, W., Crist, T. and Presley, L. (1995) 'Partnerships for Productivity', *Training and Development*, January

Sarkis, Angela and Webster, Russell (1995) *Working in Partnership: The Probation Service and the Voluntary Sector*, The Divert Trust, London

Taylor, Marilyn (1992) *Signposts to Community Development*, Community Development Foundation, London

Temple, Peter (1994) 'Working Together', *Investors Chronicle*, Vol. 108, No. 1375, May

Tomalin, Christina and Pal, John (1994) 'Local Authority Responses to Retail Change', *International Journal of Retail and Distribution Management*, Vol. 22, No. 6

United Nations Environment Programme (1994) *Partnerships for Sustainable Development: The role of Business and Industry*, The Prince of Wales Business Leaders Forum, London

Wesson, Will (1993) 'Creating Cities that Work: Managing Partnership', *Education and Training*, Vol. 36, No. 6

Whitelaw, The Rt Hon Viscount KT CH MC (1995) *The Arnold Goodman Charity Lecture Report*, The Charities Aid Foundation, Tonbridge, Kent, 6 June

Wilcox, David (1994a) *The Guide to Effective Participation*, Partnership Books, Brighton

Wilcox, David (1994b) *The A to Z of Partnerships*, Paper for New Cities '94: Conference on Urban Regeneration and Community Participation, the Economic Policy Team of the National Council for Voluntary Organisations, March